BECOMING
THE BEST

9 SECRETS FOR
STEPPING INTO GREATNESS

BECOMING
THE BEST

9 SECRETS FOR
STEPPING INTO GREATNESS

PHINEHAS KINUTHIA

Becoming the Best You: 9 Secrets for Stepping into Greatness
Copyright © 2019 by Dreaming to Becoming, LLC

Use of italics in quotations is author's emphasis.
Book Cover Designed by: Global Deziners
Edited & Formatted by: Hunter Entertainment Network
Editors: Erin Brown and Deborah Hunter

ISBN (Paperback): 978-1-937741-02-0
Printed in the United States of America.

DEDICATION

~To my daughter, Claire, and my son, Luke, from the first time your mom and I set our eyes on you and held you, we realized that you were both destined for greatness and that you both possessed something extraordinary. Through the years, you have continued to live up to that expectation, as we see you develop and grow into amazing young people who continue to provide incentives for me to pursue my dreams. It's my desire that the words in this book will awaken a desire in you to be all you were purposed to be in life, that you will stretch beyond your limitations and the boundaries of your environment, and that you will dare to go where Mom and I have not gone and attain more than we have or ever will.

~To my wife, Joyce, thank you for the sacrifices you have made, for believing in me, and for encouraging me as I pursue my dreams.

~To my family, thank you for your faith in me, your belief in my dreams, your encouragement and challenging me to go further.

~To all my personal mentees and protégé's around the world whom I have had the privilege to equip, train, develop, and empower to step into your greatness.

~To all others whom I have had the honor and opportunity to impact directly or indirectly through my inspirational messages or my books.

~To everyone with a dream who wants to activate their potential and aspire to move from mere "dreaming to becoming."

FOREWORD

Over the last couple of years, I have had the distinct pleasure of co-founding and helping to move forward a global initiative focused on building cultures of honor. As such, it is my great privilege to endorse *"Becoming the Best You"* by Dr. Phinehas Kinuthia. Dr. Kinuthia has a deep and true understanding of what it means to honor the essence of who we are and in *Becoming the Best You*, he expresses time-worn, effective approaches to achieve this.

I believe that one of the great tragedies of our modern times is that we have too frequently forfeited our natural-born, God-given gifts – this in pursuit of trendy, topic-of-the-moment characteristics, limited application skills, or fleeting fame and social significance. In addition, in seeking to build public profile and status, we frequently forego reasoning and thinking skills. Further, we expect immediate results and lofty achievements without a willingness to do the hard work or make the sacrifices that almost anything worth having takes to accomplish.

Failing to become our best selves by recognizing, utilizing, and honoring our gifts comes at a tremendous cost to human-kind. Dr. Kinuthia offers nine best practices for managing our lives and gifts that each of us can engage in to ensure we find our best selves and avoid the cost and consequences that go along with mediocrity, complacency, and hopelessness. Dr. Kinuthia reminds us that among other things, adopting simple disciplines, honoring our histories, being true to our core values, and thinking differently are secrets to stepping into our greatness.

The section of the book that addresses "followershift" resonated with me in a particularly powerful way. I strongly agree with Dr. Phinehas's assertion that we live in a time where inauthentic leadership has become the norm and in the absence of men and women willing to follow first, we find ourselves inhibiting opportunities and potential for true leadership. I encourage you to open the covers of this book with a teachable attitude and with a learning mindset. Doing so will enable you to unlock your full capacity to become the best you.

Becoming the Best You is one of those books so chalk full of timeless, practical information and strategies that you will re-read it over and over. Thank you, Phinehas, for sharing your wisdom and insight; this is a legacy book that my children and my children's children will pass along and reference on their journeys to becoming their best selves.

Dr. Lewena Bayer, CEO
Civility Experts Inc & Co-Founder of Golden Rule Civility

ENDORSEMENTS

Dr. Phinehas Kinuthia is one of the most prolific writers with a true understanding of leadership and human potential that I've ever heard in my life. This book will truly solve problems of this world at the core level, if we endeavor to follow and engage these nine secrets for stepping into greatness and awaken the best versions of ourselves and those we lead. Every leader in the world needs to read this masterpiece.

World Peace Leader
Ambassador Dr. Clyde Rivers, Representative to the United Nations

A dream is an "I wish" statement. But a dream does not become real until there is a commitment, a plan, and a great deal of persistence no matter what obstacles a person faces. Phinehas Kinuthia has provided a solid roadmap to develop and stay focused on that plan to make a life dream a true reality and help you move towards greatness.

Brad Smith
President, Bakke Graduate University

"Becoming the Best You" is a recommended must read for all, skillfully and divinely written by Dr. Phinehas Kinuthia. This book not only demonstrates that there's a clear and direct path out of the everyday ruts of life, but it also provides the process.

Van W. Johnson, Sr.
Mayor of Apalachicola, Florida

Greatness... Potential... Purpose... all somewhat overused phrases in today's pop-psychology-driven world of personal development. Indeed, we are not wandering generalities. God has placed greatness within each one of us. But, how to live that out remains every pilgrim's quest. My friend Dr. Kinuthia has written a book that goes beyond conventional treatment of this critical subject. He gives us a clear roadmap to unlocking potential. Read it, and re-read it, then boldly walk these secrets out. May you become!

Dr. Dennis D. Sempebwa
President & CEO Sahara Wisdom Center Dallas, TX

Dr. Phinehas Kinuthia has written a book sumptuously prepared, but remarkably clear. I highly recommend it for those serious about maximizing the likelihood of personal success. This book is further recommended for the rich and informative wisdom it offers from convergent disciplines. It lays a comprehensive foundation for a subsequent annotated bibliography on related topics. BECOMING THE BEST IN YOU disturbs complacent models and asserts intentional action in order to be purposeful in living. I recommend it as a thoroughly engaging perspective for improving all too often ignored areas of both individual and civic conduct. The author's tone is simultaneously conversational and emphatic - creating a motivation to change.

Cynthia Rembert James, PhD., D.Min.
Associate Pastor, The Potters House Dallas

Dr. Phinehas Kinuthia's BECOMING THE BEST YOU is an insightful book full of tools to guide leaders, professionals, and everyday influencers on the journey of unleashing the greatness in them and others. Not only is his message relevant to many people who would read the book, but he also does a great job of making a powerful call to action that engages the reader in their own journey of becoming their best version. This book is beyond inspiring and will move you to action. A must-read, especially for those who desire to step into the future with courage, determination, and mission to fulfill and live in their ultimate purpose.

Dr. Margaret Ellis, PhD
Author, CEO/Brand Ambassador – Coaches of Influence

In our quest for becoming the best version of ourselves, most people often negate the mindset and logistical steps necessary in the process. Phinehas Kinuthia provides the tools to not only connect-the-dots of implementation, but also provides a much-needed paradigm shift that will help you move into greatness.

Susan Nichols
Connecting Communities Consulting

Dr. Phinehas Kinuthia's BECOMING THE BEST YOU is a uniquely insightful book. It clearly lays before the reader the unveiling of secrets for an ordinary individual to tread toward greatness. It is more than a "self-help" book; it is a self-hope book! BECOMING THE BEST YOU answers the questions of life's purpose and challenges the reader to take the steps to becoming their best, not the best someone else. I whole-heartedly recommend it as a catalyst for one's authentic achievement.

Dr. John D. Ogletree, Jr.
Senior Pastor, First Metropolitan Church, Houston, TX

Dr. Phinehas Kinuthia is an absolutely excellent writer and communicator. I love to read books that I can "hear" the voice of the author without it sounding mundane and "robotic," if you will. *Becoming the Best You* speaks to the hearts of humanity to dig deeper and seek further why they were created, in a manner in which ALL can receive.

Deborah G. Hunter
Hunter Entertainment Network

Phinehas Kinuthia has scripted and excellent formula for personal success. He clearly outlines the process of moving from ordinary to extra-ordinary with insight and precision. Many of us want to be great, but are not prepared to do what it takes to achieve personal greatness. BECOMING THE BEST YOU eliminates excuses for not becoming the best you possible through simple proven principles that when applied, will lead to an improved attitude, improved thinking skills, and improved outcome. You will be thoroughly challenged and inspired as you read.

Dave Burrows
BFMI International, Nassau Bahamas

ACKNOWLEDGEMENTS

Nothing worthwhile is accomplished alone, for it is always a result of collaborative effort with others. The writing of this book is a result of such effort. I have gleaned the wisdom of other successful individuals who've inspired my life, and challenged and motivated me in many ways over the years. These thought leaders have helped me learn and develop new philosophies and ideologies, while helping me to explore new paradigms of thought and cultivate these secrets that I am able to share with you in this book.

To my inner circle that have supported this project and made this project a reality, you are exceptional. I am forever grateful for your input and uncommon investment in me and my dreams. It truly takes a dream team to make the dream work.

To my brother Charles, whose unrelenting passion and motivation has kept me on my feet working countless hours to ensure that this project is completed on time and with excellence.

To my editor, Erin Brown, thank you for the amazing hard work and dedication in helping me get this message across to my audience effectively.

TABLE OF CONTENTS

INTRODUCTION

Death is inevitable. When you die, what will be your legacy? How do you want to be remembered? What will be your epitaph? Have you lived a life of significance, making an impression on your world and other people?

Are you exhausted by existing on the periphery of success, while never fully accomplishing anything of importance? Are you increasingly discontented with maintaining the status quo? How do you assess your current accomplishments? Do your accomplishments influence other people's lives? Are you living effectively or are you living in obscurity?

How long will you continue to accommodate mediocrity at the expense of your full potential? How many people have bypassed you and become successful, while you remain wishing that something great will happen to you? Do you long to see your life transformed? Do you desire change that will move you toward greatness? How strong is your desire to break out of your comfort zone and increase your sphere of influence? Do you want to live a life that matters? Do you want to live a life that is extraordinary and has a lasting impact? Have you explored what the "best you" would look like? Why is the life you are living so different from the life you dream of?

These are questions you must ruminate on and honestly answer for yourself as you read *Becoming the Best You*. My hope is that you will engage with the enormous insight, tools, resources, and proven secrets of greatness I have shared in this book.

No one wakes up wishing to be ordinary, yet it seems to be the norm for the masses living in quiet desperation as they move through the ordinary tasks of life, with no sense of meaning or significance. Earl Nightingale said that most people tiptoe through life, hoping to make it safely to death. While this might be the reality for many, I believe that deep down each of us possesses a secret desire or an avid ambition to be exceptional, to make a noticeable difference in people's lives. We all want our story to count. We want to have a life of significance. We want to create an indelible impact in the lives of others. But, we don't know how. The world needs not only dreamers who want to achieve greatness, but also those who are willing to pursue and actualize their dreams at all costs.

The yearning for fulfillment and greatness is in each of us, inspiring us to take massive action and do all we are capable of in order to attain everything we were meant to be. Abraham Maslow, world famous psychologist, called this desire *self-actualization*, a desire to become everything one is capable of. He observed that anyone who sets out to be less than he is capable of will be unhappy for the rest of his or her life.

We secretly desire to be great in different areas of our lives, be it our parenting, marriages, relationships, businesses, careers, education, health, or anything of value to us. While we desire this life of significance, we should also be aware that it is not something we stumble upon. Rather, it requires a clear understanding and mastery of the steps and skills necessary to move us from *dreaming to becoming*. Just as the law of gravity governs free fall, or the law of aerodynamics determines a plane's ability for flight, everything we accomplish or achieve is a function of the laws or principles that create and govern them.

Unless we learn these principles and laws that lead to success and significance, they will work against us, instead of working for us. Ignorance of principles doesn't negate their effects. Most people don't know what it requires to connect the dots and move toward the greatness they dream of. When we recognize the desire for greatness and determine the path toward it, success rests upon our engagement with the critical disciplines, laws, principles, and tools that promise to move us consistently toward greatness. Our good intentions will never birth greatness, but only our engagement with the secrets and the passionate pursuit of the path that leads to greatness.

I wrote *Becoming the Best You* with you in mind. This book is all about developing a new way of thinking, being, and doing, which will lead you to step into your inherent greatness. The reality is that an increasing number of people today are confronted with a sad reality that they have not reached their maximum potential. If you keep doing what you have always done, you are bound to have what you have always had. My goal is not to exhaustively provide all of life's skills and secrets that lead to greatness, but we will attempt to explore the fundamental qualities and secrets that will position you on a trajectory that will accelerate your journey toward your personal greatness.

What Is Greatness?

You must identify greatness for yourself. In the words of Thomas Carlyle, "No great man lives in vain. The history of the world is but a biography of great men." You have to determine for yourself what greatness is to you. Greatness is first defined in our minds and soul, and then we pursue it until we have actualized it.

What is this clarion call to move toward greatness? Greatness is not a destination; it's a continuous state of being, a progressive achievement toward excellence and away from a life of complacency or mediocrity. It's a selfless disposition to want to rise above all you are and to becoming all you were intended to be, thus making an indelible impact on others in the process.

Greatness is elusive. It beckons us to a life of constant growth and advancement because we never really arrive, for our destination evolves with our growth.

Desire is the beginning of human achievement. Greatness is first a personal desire before it is a reality. From desire begins the drive to move from obscurity to significance, not for the sake of eminence, fame, or celebrity status, but for a genuine desire to reach your full potential and impact others' lives. Honoring your potential promises a future wrapped in greatness.

You owe it to yourself to make pursuing your ultimate potential and reaching your capacity a lifelong endeavor. Zig Ziglar said, "You don't have to be great to start, but you have to start to be great." Most people are where they are in life, because of the sum total of their decisions.

You Are Unlimited

You possess limitless potential. Greatness comes from within, not from the outside. Every manifested dream today was first an invisible thought in someone's mind. You were made for greatness, so you must develop a complete disregard for where mediocrity has held you hostage. Deep within every one of us, waiting to be revealed, are thoughts and desires for greatness.

Many people live on the periphery of greatness, never fully realizing their ultimate potential. When you discover that your potential and abilities can be developed and expanded, you can seize them and use them to pursue your dreams. Maya Angelou said, "One isn't necessarily born with courage, but one is born with potential." Everything you need to excel in life is hidden within you in potential waiting to be explored.

"Compared to what we ought to be, we are only half awake. We are making use of only a small part of our physical and mental resources. Stating the thing broadly, the human individual thus lives far within his limits. He possesses power of various sorts which he habitually fails to use."

~Sir Williams James

The ultimate human potential remains latent until a demand is laid upon it. Too many in our generation live with their potential locked deep within them. The reservoir of your potential will remain untapped and buried in the rubble of insecurity and fear, until you dig it up then exploit and maximize your potential.

A Diamond Is a Rock with Its Potential Discovered

"No individual has any right to come into the world and go out of it without leaving behind him distinct and legitimate reasons for having passed through it."

~George Washington Carver

Everyone comes into this world with unlimited potential, regardless of opportunities, geographic location, nationality, economic status, capacity, or any circumstance surrounding their birth. There will never be someone like you, with the same combination of talents, abilities, desires, skills, personality, dreams, perception, imagination, and potential. To subject yourself to someone else's potential can destroy your opportunity for greatness. Therefore, failing to develop and maximize your potential is denying the world your uniqueness and solutions to humanity's problems. You have an inherent ability conferred to you to accomplish your assignment. God did His part in depositing your potential into you; now, do your part in releasing your potential.

Are You Ready?

You have a choice right now to keep reading this book or to put it down before you read any further. If you decide to keep reading, be advised that you are about to engage your life like you have never done before. You will explore life-changing truths. Be warned that this book will shake you out of the confines of your comfort and push you out of the nest of your ease. You are about to learn how to change the way you live. Through the insights you will gain from reading this book, you will apply small changes in your life that will eventually bring about a huge impact—little hinges of change that swing open the big doors to greatness.

I know you might be questioning if this book is worth your time. I have been there, trying to decide whether or not to purchase a book and if it would help me accomplish my dreams. I grew tired of reading books that give information about greatness, but offer no practical or executable and actionable steps to bring about personal transformation. There is a reason most *how-to* books don't seem to work. If we focus on steps only and not understanding the philosophy behind the action, we fail to adopt the required behavior and therefore fail to experience the results we hoped for. We need the right mindset to birth the right results.

If you think you can skim these chapters and pick up the essence of the content, you will miss out on the treasure buried within the pages. I did not write this book for the "expert," even though they can learn a lot from it. I wrote *Becoming the Best You* for the hungry person who, regardless of his or her background or status, has a longing to move toward greatness.

My utmost desire is that this book will not only inform you, but ignite your passion, spark your inspiration, and awaken your desire, so that you will use these practical, actionable tools to help you navigate the challenges of life, the ebb and flow of your being, with true-north principles and proven skills that push you toward greatness. I believe it's your time to write your name in the chapters of history. This is your moment to be more, to reach higher, and to go farther than you ever thought possible. This is your time to rise above the masses and be distinct. Decide right now, with unwavering commitment, that you will become the best in all you set out to be and develop yourself into accomplishing your maximum potential.

1

DISCOVER YOUR CORE

"This is the soulful meaning of happiness: to live the life that is truly ours, to give the most of who we essentially are."

~Jack Weber

The year is 1993, in Nakuru, Kenya a remote African town where a little malnourished boy is playing soccer outside with other kids. The boy had been born premature, weighing two pounds at birth and had struggled in early childhood with some developmental issues, asthma attacks, and chronic bronchitis. Despite his early challenges, the boy strived to be part of the game. Perhaps emulating or mimicking his heroes, fancifully dreaming of one day becoming a great player like the Argentinean superstar at the time named Diego Maradona. The soccer ball the children played with was not a real soccer ball; rather, it was a make-shift lump of paper and plastic woven together by a thread. The goal posts were stones conveniently positioned equidistant to one another on opposite ends of the road. All the other kids seemed to be having fun without a sense of care in the world. To them it was just another day in their own paradise. They were sweating it out on the street, while watching out for any oncoming traffic to avoid being hit by any vehicles shuffling through the dusty roads used as the pitch.

A few months prior to the soccer game, the little boy had a near death experience. He had contracted a disease known as typhoid fever caused by contaminated food or water. During that time, there was no running water in the town requiring most people to fetch water from community wells or purchase unclean water from water pods. At the same time, the little boy also contracted malaria. These two new diseases complicated the boy's existing struggle with asthma and chronic bronchitis attacks. Deaths from less severe conditions were common. The little boy's situation was dire. The boy was rushed to the clinic, yet there were insufficient medical resources to diagnose or properly treat his conditions. The doctors provided what they could only to discover that the injection offered had left the boy paralyzed on his left side causing the inability to walk. For several days, the boy lived in fear and devastation, traumatized by not knowing whether he would ever walk again. As the young boy suffered, he began to ask questions about life. Why had fate chosen this path for an already sick young child who had no means to make his life any different or better? This was a little too much to comprehend for a young child. Fortunately, three days after the paralysis, by an act of divine intervention, the boy was healed. Perhaps because the medicine wore out of his body or as a result of an act of God, or what many might reference to as *healing*. He regained his ability to walk and take part in the neighborhood soccer game.

Each of us can be traumatized by certain experiences. Whenever trauma strikes, especially near-death incidents, it can force us to reflect. Soon after the trauma, the young boy started asking himself questions, why had life ordered these significant blows and tragedy? Was there anything better in life for him or was he relegated to a life of poverty, deprivation, and pain? It seemed as though other people had it made and that the only way one would succeed was to be born with an upper hand in life?

It was during that season of uncertainty and devastation a friend stopped by to visit the boy and gave him an inspirational message. In the message (which was a VHS video tape similar to DVD today) was a story of someone who had overcome extreme difficulties in life. The character in the film had also been born disenfranchised in a third world country, was the seventh of twelve siblings, and lived in a two roomed house with his family. The family was without any rich relatives, yet the character overcame all odds by becoming a great global leader. The message spoke to this little boy and brought a sense of self awareness and purpose. He realized that it wasn't really what was happening to him, where he was born, or the circumstances surrounding him that marked his fate; rather, how he responded to life that mattered. Soon, the young boy began to seek out ways he could change his life for the better and possibly have a better chance of attaining his lofty dreams. Perhaps not being a famous soccer player, but amounting to something significant. That little boy in the story is me. This journey brought me to awareness that everything existing had a sense of meaning and purpose and that my job was to discover and live out that sense of purpose to find fulfillment. I realized several years ago that life loses its meaning without the understanding of the very essence of one's own existence or what is also known as the *core* of one's existence. Unless we have a strong compelling understanding of why we exist, we will not know our reason for being. Understanding one's self and the core of one's existence can mean the difference between success and failure. It is what brings freedom and significance into one's life.

It is impossible for individuals, or an organization, to reach their full potential and achieve great things without first defining the core of their existence. Who we are is our core, the axis from around which our entire lives revolve. Without determining our core, we cannot make significant progress in attaining success, or tap into our ultimate potential, or moving from obscurity to greatness. Everything you were meant to be originates from the core of who you were created to be.

The core of your existence is the unique, divine, total essence of who you ought to be, your value system, what you ought to do—the reason why you exist on earth.

Your core is the original *you* as intended by your Maker in the same manner as how a manufacturer determines the purpose and use of a product. The core of your existence is the desired result, intent, or outcome; it answers the *why* you are here. The core of existence is never independent of design, just as the specifications of a product determine its design. In this chapter, we will refer to the core of your existence as "Your Core."

Dr. Phillip C. McGraw in *Self Matters*, in which he writes about finding your authentic self, states,

> The authentic self is the *you* that can be found at the absolute core. It is the part of you that is not defined by your job, or your function, or your role. It is the composite of all your unique gifts, skills, abilities, interests, talents, insights, and wisdom. It is all your strengths and values that are uniquely yours and need expression, versus what you have been pro-grammed to believe you are 'supposed' to be and do.[1]

Most precious metals and gemstones are formed below the earth's surface, hidden from view. To extract them requires mining through several inches to hundreds of feet of dirt and rock. Similar-ly, we all have treasure hidden within us, buried in ordinariness and valuable only when discovered. The great Italian sculptor, painter, architect, and poet Michelangelo once said, "In every block of marble I see a statue as plain as though it stood before me, shaped and perfect in attitude and action. I have only to hew away the rough walls that imprison the lovely apparition to reveal it to the other eyes as mine see it." It's our relentless pursuit in the discovery of our purpose that chips away and extracts the treasure within us.

We all have treasure hidden within us, buried in ordinariness and valuable only when discovered.

What is your Core?

Let's begin by exploring this question: What is your core? Understanding your core will help you discover the jewel inside you, where your deposit of potential lies. Real life can only be realized from the core of who you are. Your external life and its realities emerge from and find its existence from your core. Most people mistakenly define themselves by what they do: their career, education, or personal accomplishments. When the stage lights are off, the show is over, and you stop doing what you do, you must know who you are—your core that's not defined by what you do. Do you know who you are?

The search for the meaning of life and the origin of humanity's existence has been the center of many philosophical debates. Most people are constantly searching for the meaning of their lives, seeking to know what their contribution to life is. Some try to replace this persistent longing with material things: the cars they drive or the houses they live in or the clothes they wear. Others desire to find value in their careers or their businesses. Some seek ultimate fulfillment in their marriages, families, or friends. Religions have been started as a byproduct of the quest for significance and the meaning of existence.

Every human has an inherent secret desire to realize the core of their existence.

In an attempt to fulfill their aspirations, some people become frustrated because they try too hard being what they were never equipped to be. It may be that they believe the reason for their existence is the result of chance or fate, that their destiny has already been determined and sealed by circumstances beyond their control. Or, in their desperate search for a meaningful life, they keep changing directions, jobs, relationships, and even lifestyles; yet, their problems and emptiness follow them wherever they go. Those who fear the uncertainty of the outcome of a rigorous quest for their purpose acquiesce to a mundane life as a safe, though dull, alternative. One who never becomes what he or she was born to be can never be counted successful. Even if a person is great at what he was never meant to be, he is still a great failure.

"The heart of human excellence often begins to beat when you discover a pursuit that absorbs you, frees you, challenges you, or gives you a sense of meaning, joy, or passion."

~Terry Orlick

What you do and the success you realize is irrelevant if you fail to understand why you are doing it. Knowing who you are and what you are about will help you not to waste time trying to be what you were never meant to be.

For example, before a business launches, the owners develop a business plan that will steer them toward success. They answer questions like these: Why does this business exist? What is the purpose of the business? What will the business do that others are not doing or cannot do? Knowing this will keep the business on track doing what it was designed to do, and it will keep it from drifting into activities, products, or services it is not equipped to do. In the same way, answering these kinds of questions before you pursue a direction will help you to identify the reason for your existence and pursue those things that coincide with your essential self.

Your pursuit and discovery of your core can also be understood much easily by delving into what's important to you or to your organization. The belief system or ideas that are very central to whom you are, and those that shape what you value the most. It is what you are not willing to live without or the ideas or ideals you want to live by at any cost that shape who you are and help define your core.

The truth is your reason for being is not a decision, but a discovery. To discover your reason for being, you must go beyond what's visible. It's a search that must reach into your inner core.

"And now here is my secret, a very simple secret: it is only with the heart that one can see rightly; what is essential is invisible to the eye."
~Antoine de Saint-Exupéry

To be indomitable, you must know your Creator's original intent—*Your Core*. Nothing in your life is arbitrary or coincidental; everything about you has a plan and is purposeful, complex, and significant.

Let me assure you that what I am about to share is not an attempt to persuade you to matters of faith or religion; rather, it's simply a reflection of my observation regarding life and the pursuit of greatness. I suppose that if you don't believe in God, you may come to a different conclusion and call it what you want. It is only logical that in an attempt to explore our ultimate human potential, we address the existence of an infinite being with superior power to deposit a latent potential in its creation.

If you will indulge me for just a moment, a common philosophical argument proving the existence of God is known as the Kalam Cosmological Argument, which states, "Everything that begins to exist has a cause of its existence. The universe began to exist; therefore, the universe has a cause of its existence. If the universe has a cause of its existence then that cause is God; therefore, God exists."[2] Using this premise, we could also say that because you exist, you also have a cause for your existence, and this cause must have been decided by God.

"Unless you assume a God, the question of life's purpose is meaningless."

~Bertrand Russell, Atheist

A parable told by a Hungarian writer expresses the argument well:

In a mother's womb were two babies. One asked the other, "Do you believe in life after delivery?"

The other replied, "Why, of course. There has to be something after delivery. Maybe we are here to prepare ourselves for what we will be later."

"Nonsense" the first said. "There is no life after delivery. What kind of life would that be?"

The second said, "I don't know, but there will be more light than here. Maybe we will walk with our legs and eat from our mouths. Maybe we will have other senses that we can't understand now."

The first replied, "That is absurd. Walking is impossible. And eating with our mouths? Ridiculous! The umbilical cord supplies nutrition and everything we need. But the umbilical cord is so short. Life after delivery is to be logically excluded."

The second insisted, "Well, I think there is something, and maybe it's different than it is here. Maybe we won't need this physical cord anymore."

The first replied, "Nonsense. And moreover, if there is life, then why has no one ever come back from there? Delivery is the end of life, and in the after-delivery, there is nothing but darkness and silence and oblivion. It takes us nowhere."

"Well, I don't know," said the second, "but certainly we will meet Mother and She will take care of us."

The first replied, "Mother? You actually believe in Mother? That's laughable. If Mother exists then where is She now?"

The second said, "She is all around us. We are surrounded by her. We are of Her. It is in Her that we live. Without Her this world would not and could not exist."

The first said, "Well, I don't see Her, so it is only logical that She doesn't exist."

To which the second replied, "Sometimes, when you're in silence and you focus and you really listen, you can perceive Her presence, and you can hear Her loving voice calling down from above."[3]

~Útmutató a Léleknek

It All Starts Here

Ancient scriptures reveal this truth: "That everything above and below, visible and invisible, everything got started in him and find its purpose in Him."[4] Most people are uncomfortable to talk about God. It's what some refer to as "religion," and they treat a discussion about God as private matter. While I do respect that, and I do not desire to impose my beliefs on anyone, I have come to an unequivocal decision that it all starts and ends with God. It is our denial of God and His existence that further complicates the search and meaning for life, because when we endeavor to search within ourselves outside of God, we enter an infinite maze of never-ending questions, as we try to make sense of something that is beyond our physical realm of existence, just like the twins in the parable.

An infinite being cannot be explained through finite under-standing, so humans are incapable of explaining and defining God completely. Such was my encounter that in my pursuit of my essential self, I was driven to a place of revelation that there exists a higher purpose for my existence beyond my ambitions, desires, career, dreams, or goals in life. You and I are here on earth to fulfill a unique plan determined by a Creator.

Mere existence is not the goal of life, but rather the passionate pursuit and fulfillment of a Sovereign plan for ones' life.

In his book *Man's Search for Meaning*, Viktor Frankl, a Holocaust survivor who endured unspeakable horrors in a Nazi death camp, wrote about survival.

> What was really needed was a fundamental change in our attitude toward life. We had to learn ourselves, and furthermore, we had to teach the despairing men that it did not really matter what we expected from life but rather what life expected of us. Life ultimately means taking the responsibility to find the right answer to its problems and to fulfill the tasks which it constantly set for each individual. This task and therefore the meaning of life, differ from man to man.[5]

Each of us has a task for which we are uniquely designed, and that task is determined outside of our influence and control. Rick Warren sums it up in *The Purpose Driven Life*, "You exist only because God wills that you exist. You were made by God and for God—and until you understand that, life will never make sense. It is only in God that we discover our origin, our identity, our meaning, our purpose, our significance and our destiny. Every other path leads to a dead end."[6]

It will be merely impossible of us to move from mediocrity and obscurity to greatness without clearly starting with identifying our core. To go from one place to the next, we need to know our starting point; otherwise, we will be lost. I hate being lost and not knowing where I am going. Whenever I take a trip, I must know my destination before I ever start the journey. Whenever I am at an airport or a mall or other large facility, I visit the directory to establish where I am and, based on my purpose for being there, where I want to go. On my recent trip to Minnesota, I visited the Mall of America, which is roughly 4.2 million square feet. It is the largest mall in North America. The first thing I did when I arrived was visit the directory to establish where I was; from there, I could figure out how to get where I wanted to go. If I had ignored the map and depended upon random chance, that is, wandering in hopes of getting where I needed to be, I would have gotten lost (and possibly still be there aimlessly drifting and never making progress).

Our quest to discover our essential selves begins by finding out who we are at our core. Start by asking, "Who am I, and where do I want to go in life?" You can't understand where you are going in life, until you know where you are. To know where you are, you have to locate yourself within the master builder's blueprint—the Master's plan—for our lives. Just like the directory in the mall, everything you need to know and everywhere you need to go can be located in your Creator's plan, which is where you need to be.

Who Are You?

You are not God's afterthought but His forethought, the optimal expression of His creative capacity.

We all claim some form of identity. When you were born, your parents gave you a name as part of your identity. Most adults carry some form of proof of identification. If a police officer pulls you over while driving, you could identify yourself as Joe Smith, but the officer will ask to see your driver's license. Even though you stated the truth, the officer still wants to see a government-issued identification. This is because in the eyes of the world, we really aren't who we say we are, until an authority confirms it. Our essential self is who we truly are at the core, which we received from the ultimate authority: God.

To establish your ultimate human potential, you cannot compare yourselves with other people, because you are a uniquely inspired masterpiece. A masterpiece is always an original, one-of-a-kind and is not a copy. You are one of a kind. You are special. You are significant. You are not an accident; you were meant to be. Your gifts and talents, your skills, abilities, interest, personality, strengths, wisdom, as well as your weaknesses and experiences all are specific and germane to your uniqueness. *Your uniqueness is tailored for your assignment.* You have to settle once and for all a few things in order to fully go after your ultimate potential: You are not the wrong gender, or the wrong race, or even the wrong height. You were not born in the wrong place or to the wrong family. It's not that you are not smart enough or skilled enough, fast enough or strong enough. Embrace the truth that you are a divinely inspired masterpiece who is authentically designed to complete the assignment you were created to accomplish on earth.

You are a divinely inspired masterpiece who is authentically designed to complete the assignment you were created to accomplish on earth.

Sometimes, people may say things about you or do things that tend to make you question your worth. But what your grandparents, dad and mom, siblings, uncles and aunts, teachers, or anyone else says or does doesn't change the value of who you are. Maybe, you've mistakenly developed a faulty perception of yourself that has diminished your value. The truth is, your essential core uniquely defines your value. The empowerment within you is proportionate to your assignment in life. You are who you are so you can accomplish the assignment God has given you. It does no good to compare yourself with others, because your assignment is unique to you. No one in the world has similar experiences, upbringing, genetics, perception, or ability to fulfill your mission the same exact way you can. You are uniquely and distinctively designed to be the *best you* and to accomplish the specific assignment determined by your Creator. The more precise and certain you are about your purpose, the greater the chances that you will accomplish your mission. Comparing yourself with others limits your ability to pursue and achieve everything God intends for you. Don't evaluate yourself by other people's standards but by the accomplishments you have made relative to your life's assignment.

DISCOVER YOUR CORE

"To be yourself in a world that is constantly trying to make you something else is the greatest accomplishment."

~Ralph Waldo Emerson

Your life should begin and end with *Your Core*. You cannot discover your ultimate human potential without pursuing the core of your existence. Your dream and all your pursuits must be tied to your core. Many times, you may feel the pressure to do what other people expect you to do, but endeavor to discover Your Core and build your dream around it. You will never experience greatness without discovering Your Core and building your life around it. When you discover Your Core, you will automatically know where to find fulfillment in life.

Discover Your Core Exercise

Ask yourself these thought-provoking questions to jump-start the process of discovering Your Core.

1. Why am I here?
2. Who am I, and what defines me?
3. What comes naturally to me that I am good at?
4. What are my God-given abilities, talents, strengths, and skills or dominant gifts?
5. What makes me different or distinguishes me from others?
6. What is the time you were at your best and why?
7. What is one thing I consistently and effortlessly do that impacts others?
8. What do people think I am good at and praise me for?
9. What do I feel totally passionate about—what do I love to do the most?
10. Who would I be or what would I do if my life were perfect?
11. What have I persistently been intrigued with the most throughout my childhood and adulthood, which makes me forget the world around me?
12. What is it that electrifies me and or excites me that I would love doing all the time if I could?
13. What legacy do I want to leave if I had a year to live? What do I want to accomplish within my lifetime and be remembered for?

14. What makes me feel good, smile, laugh and brings happiness and fulfillment?

15. What's the consistent driving force in my life?

16. What are my core values or what do I care deeply about?

17. What are my long-term persistent wishes and dreams I have always aspired to see fulfilled in my lifetime?

18. What do I feel is my meaningful contribution on earth, which will be written on my epitaph?

19. What do I like to work with? (For example, do you like to work with music, a computer, people, or art? These are clues you should not ignore.)

20. What problems do I absolutely hate and would love to see eradicated?

PHINEHAS'S AXIOMS

- Everything you were meant to be originates from the core of who you were created to be.
- The core of your existence is the unique, divine, total essence of who you ought to be, what you ought to do—it's the reason why you exist on earth.
- Every human has an inherent secret desire to realize the core of their existence.
- We all have treasure hidden within us, buried in ordinariness and valuable only when discovered.
- Knowing who you are and what you are about will help you not to waste time trying to be someone you were never meant to be.
- To discover your reason for being who you are, you must go beyond what's visible. It's a search that must reach your inner core.
- Understanding your core will help you discover the jewel inside you, where your deposit of potential lies.
- Nothing in your life is arbitrary or coincidental; everything about you has a plan and is purposeful, complex, and significant.
- Mere existence is not the goal of life, but rather the passionate pursuit and fulfillment of God's sovereign plan for ones' life.
- Your quest to discover your essential self begins by finding out who you are at your core.

- You are uniquely and distinctively designed to be the *best you* and to accomplish your specific assignment as determined by your Creator.
- In order to establish your ultimate human potential, you cannot compare yourself with other people, because you are each a uniquely inspired masterpiece.
- Your uniqueness is tailored for your assignment.
- You are not God's afterthought, but his forethought; the optimal expression of His creative ability.
- You are a divinely inspired masterpiece who is authentically designed to complete the assignment you were created to accomplish here on earth.
- Your essential self is who you truly are at the core, which you received from the ultimate authority: God.
- Your essential core uniquely defines your value.
- The empowerment within you is proportionate to your assignment in life.
- Don't evaluate your success by other people's standards, but by the accomplishments you have made relative to your life's assignment.

2

> ❖ <

HABITUAL ATTITUDE ADJUSTMENT

"Without a positive attitude, you can't activate the other principles. Your success in life begins and ends with your attitude. Attitude is everything!"

~Jeff Keller

An old man fell asleep in his living room. His grandchildren decided to play a trick on him. While he was asleep, they put a piece of Limburger cheese on his moustache. When the old man woke up, he was taken aback by the smell in the room, so he moved into another room. The smell was there too, but the stench was even worse. "Something in this house stinks!"

He stepped out of his house to catch some fresh air, but the odor was outside too. "This whole world stinks!" The man yelled loud enough for the neighbors to hear.

It never occurred to him that the source of the stink was the Limburger cheese on his moustache. Unless we deal with what's in us, we will blame the world around us, while the real issue is our attitude. A good attitude is a fragrance, but a bad attitude is a stench.

The Power of Attitude

I will never forget when I landed my first job interview through a work-force agency in 2002. Prior to this event, I had only worked in a school kitchen cafeteria washing dishes and flipping burgers. This would be my first office job and as a young man moving up the ranks, I was excited. The position was for a credit card debt collector in one of the largest collection agencies in the USA that has since gone out of business. As an African, I was advancing in the pursuit of my American dream. This was a dream come true for me, because I was going to earn at least ten dollars an hour, significantly more than my previous pay which was $6.25. I was so excited to land an opportunity that I did not even prepare for the interview. In retrospect, if I was the hiring manager, I could not have hired me.

My naivety and inexperience with a corporate interview left me little to go on regarding what or how to prepare. The morning of the interview, I woke up and I chose the best burgundy suit I could find that I later discovered was clearly not in compliance with the dress code. I had my résumé prepared and I knew that I was going to land a great office job. When the manager, Mr. Marcus arrived, I introduced myself with a firm handshake and looked at him straight in the eye. Although at the time I was shy and not very confident, I attempted to the best of my ability to answer his questions and engage him in a conversation. Since I was not familiar with the job, I had to 'pitch' myself to him. I remember my words to him were, "I might not have experience and a lack of experience is not an inability. I have what you are looking for, I am a quick study, I can learn this and because I am teachable, you can expect within the next ninety days, I will be one of your top employees. You give me ninety days and if I don't deliver, you are free to fire me no questions asked."

One of the questions I recall being asked (which I laugh so hard about today) was how many times I thought I would be tardy? Now, being born and raised in Africa, English was not my first language and tardy is not really a common word. I thought Mr. Marcus asked how many times I would be tidy to which I replied, "every day." He looked at me with surprise on his face and started laughing hysterically. Still unaware of the meaning of tardy, I continued to humor Mr. Marcus by saying "No, I was being funny, maybe twice a week." Eventually, after some more laughter, the misinterpretation was resolved. At the end of the interview Mr. Marcus said, "I like you. I have interviewed several more qualified individuals than you, but you have a great attitude and I want to give you a chance. I will hire you to be on my team and I will train you." What I lacked in skill and experience, I made up in a positive attitude.

One of the greatest influences of potential is attitude. Nothing is as powerful as attitude in shaping your character and developing the ability to pursue and reach your potential in life. It's attitude that distinguishes leaders from followers. The most identifiable quality of a champion is an overall winning attitude. Attitude separates winners from losers. It is attitude that determines the ability to succeed or fail. Attitude dictates your response to the present and shapes your expectation of the future. Attitude is contagious and can affect relationships. Even organizations and businesses demonstrate their attitude through their approach toward their clients or customers. From some of the greatest global achievements to the most incredible personal accomplishments, the one force that compels individuals or organizations to penetrate beyond human odds and countless barriers is attitude. High achievers and consistently motivated people are always people with a great attitude.

It is not so much skill that determines one's ability to climb the highest mountain; rather, it's one's attitude to overcome all the obstacles and scale that mountain.

Success starts and ends with the right attitude. In fact, you are incapable of manifesting your full, unlimited potential without a great positive attitude toward life. Many opportunities are lost, withheld, or acquired because of one's attitude. Those who seek to be great emergent leaders must work on their attitudes; a change in attitude is a change in life. A positive attitude is a passport or visa to greater opportunities. It can take you to places you want to go or places you never intended to go. The right attitude unlocks doors, but the wrong attitude closes doors. Your ability to advance from obscurity to greatness and realize your ultimate human potential is influenced more by your attitude than your aptitude or attributes.

"Your attitude and your potential go hand in hand."

~John Maxwell

Consider the lion. It's not the tallest animal in the jungle; nor is it the heaviest. It is neither the smartest nor the strongest animal in the jungle. However, the lion is referred to as *the king of the jungle*, a leader, because of its attitude. A leader's performance and success is greatly influenced by his or her attitude—even more than his or her attributes.

Attitude is a choice you make; it is not an attribute. It's very possible to do the right thing with the wrong attitude. No amount of skill, expertise, or knowledge, and regardless of the number of titles that follow your name can replace a lack of right attitude. In other words, you are not compelled by instinct, as is the king of the jungle, to see things a certain way; rather, your response to events, situations, and people is a choice you make that's influenced by your disposition.

"Ability is what you're capable of doing. Motivation determines what you do. Attitude determines how well you do it."

~Lou Holtz

What Is Attitude?

I believe that attitude is influenced by a self-portrait of who we think we are or what we think we are not. Right or wrong attitudes come from our pattern of thinking about people, events past or present, which affects and influences our behaviors, feelings, or mood and consequently impacts our approach or action in response toward them.

- Psychologists define attitudes as, "A learned tendency to evaluate things in a certain way. This can include evaluations of people, issues, objects, or events. Such evaluations are often positive or negative, but they can also be uncertain at times."[1]
- "Attitude is really about how a person is that overflows into how he acts."[2]
- "Think of attitude as the mental filter through which you experience the world. Some people experience the world through the filter of optimism, while others see the life through the filter of pessimism. Your attitude is your window to the world."[3]

How Attitudes Form

Attitudes are formed over a long period of time and may develop from several factors.

Experiences

One factor that shapes attitudes is *experiences*; both positive and negative experiences significantly affect our lives and have a greater impact in influencing our attitudes. Take for instance a person who grew up in poverty. The experience of poverty can influence her to believe that she is a second-class citizen when she compares herself with wealthy people. Social classes perpetuate these beliefs and alienate the human potential of many people who have experienced poverty. This significantly affects one's approach to life and, ultimately, his attitude unless someone can reframe past negative experiences into a catalyst for personal advancement.

The attitude of someone who grew up experiencing wealth is very different. This person likely received the best training and enjoyed opportunities afforded the wealthy. He probably was constantly reassured that he could do whatever he wanted, and he was prepared to succeed in life. Though this situation is success-oriented, it can also work to the contrary. Someone who has been exposed to wealth might become predisposed to thinking that everyone and everything can be bought, that money is the "be all and end all". She might also believe that her wealth will buy her out of any trouble or any situation—assuming superiority (attitude) that her wealth will get her anything.

Environment

Environments are critical and play a major role in shaping and developing one's attitude. Where we are is a determining factor for what grows in us. The environment we were born in has a role in shaping our expectations or outlook, which affects our attitude. Certain beliefs are deeply embedded in some cultures or environments. People born in the disenfranchised, inner-city, poverty-stricken areas, affectionately known as the *hood*, may have a hard time succeeding, because they feel bound and limited to the circumstance of their environment. There is a cultural expectation from some people that those raised in such environments don't become much or end up being a product of their environment. It doesn't take much imagination to note the vastly different inherent attitudes between kids from the projects in Chicago and kids from suburbia Beverly Hills.

What we believe of ourselves might not be true, yet our environment will influence our beliefs and reinforce our attitudes, be they right or wrong.

Growing up in Africa, the instability of my environment and the lack of infrastructure made me feel inadequate, unprepared, and unable to accomplish my dreams. It felt as though anyone born in Africa was destined to fail, because the imbedded belief was that nothing good can come out of Africa. The environment seemed to support this tainted thought. Media's stereotypes reinforced the attitude that Africa is a place where people need aid, kids are orphans, and countries are full of corruption. As a result, many Africans, including myself, might tend to be intimidated by great opportunities and will, therefore, shy away from creating or innovating and building something, believing that other people are better suited to create, innovate, or build. In other words, there is a belief that others are better suited and more capable of accomplishing the opportunities they are presented with. This belief kept me from pursuing my dreams and ambitions, and as long as you feel incapable, you will always underperform, and your self-concept will always influence your self-conduct.

Outlook

Your outlook of life is contaminated by the toxicity of your inner thoughts.

According to Hugh Downs, talk show host, news anchor, and author, "A happy person is not a person in certain set of circumstances, but rather a person with certain set of attitudes." We are as happy as we choose to be, and, in the same way, we are as miserable as we choose to be. When we look at life as a victim, then suddenly we will see everyone as a perpetrator of our pain, and our attitude toward them darkens.

Do you see life from a pessimistic or optimistic attitude? How do you see your past? How do you interpret and view the present and ultimately, how do you imagine the future? It is up to you to determine how you look at life and what you expect of life around. Oscar Wilde, famous Irish poet and playwright, once said, "We are all in the gutter, but some of us are looking at the stars."

"To different minds, the same world is a hell and a heaven."

~Ralph Waldo Emerson

Wardrobe/Posture

Personal appearance always affects attitudes, as well as performances. People will address us according to the way we dress, because they tend to judge our worth through our appearance. It is said, "Don't judge a book by its cover," but it's true that people do judge others by their appearance. I do not only mean just what we wear, although this is important. I mean the way we perceive and carry ourselves. Our demeanor, the posture we assume, matters.

How we carry ourselves influences our attitudes, our feelings, and impacts how others receive us. The world is crazy about looks; people pay a premium to look and feel a certain way. Have you ever realized that when your self-confidence is high, your posture is different? People who carry a chip on their shoulders hold an attitude that someone owes them, that they are the victim. As a result, they are angry and bitter, and their attitudes toward life are negative.

An attitude adjustment is the best makeover you can do for yourself to succeed in life.

Philosophy of Life

Our philosophy of life—beliefs—greatly influences our attitude. Also, the philosophy of an organization's leader affects the attitude of the organization. Most people operate in a negative mindset. To change this, to put on a positive spirit, is to recognize that something better and greater is awaiting you. Regardless of where you are right now, there is always possibility for greater ahead. I believe we all can be more, reach higher, and go farther than we ever have. In the words of John Maxwell, "When our attitude is positive and conducive for growth, the mind expands and progress begins." Our outlook on life has to be filled with possibility that we are energized to overcome our current trials. Know that you can dream of great things. You will go farther with optimism, than you will with pessimism.

It's never about your present trials; it's always about your future triumphs.

When you believe that life is conspiring to give you the very best, you begin to expect the best; so, the best begins to gravitate toward you. Then suddenly, you see that even the small positive things that happen are steps toward the greater good in realizing the success you aspire to. It's the law of attraction that what we expect, we begin to attract towards us. On the contrary, if we believe that life is conspiring to give us the worst, then we become a magnet of unpleasant experiences. I learned that when I start the day by expecting good to come my way, little things that happen excite me: finding a parking spot in a crowded mall, or getting a discount I was not anticipating. While this might seem insignificant to some people, because I am expecting good, I make every little good thing that happens count. The attitude to "wear" at the start of every day is, "This is my day, and it is all working together for my good."

Your attitude is the weather forecast that predicts how your day will look like; learn to make it a brighter day.

Your attitude asserts your identity and influences your behavior. Your attitude acts as a mental filter or a camera lens through which you view life. When your attitude is wrong, the image is fuzzy; but when your attitude is clear, your perceptions of life are clear. It is not our circumstances that make us unhappy, but our attitude in the circumstance that will make us unhappy. Happiness is an attitude you choose and not a state of being dictated by circumstance. Your response toward life will influence how others approach you and treat you. It affects how you feel about or see things.

Possibility attitude influences courage. We must embrace this most basic belief that we are capable, and we can. There are a lot more reasons why "you can" than why "you can't". Champions behave like champions long before others recognize them as such. Champions are not born in the ring. People who win championships don't show up to the game thinking about losing. They might be afraid, but the excitement and possibility of winning makes them want to confront their opponents. You cannot approach life with a defeatism mentality and expect to conquer life's battles. You cannot think failure and act like a champion. Success or failure all starts with your attitude. Think back to your past and ask yourself: "What if I approached every opportunity with a possibility mentality?" I guarantee that you would be further along today in your journey toward greatness.

Attitude Adjustment Required

"Nothing can stop the man with the right mental attitude from achieving his goal; nothing on earth can help the man with the wrong mental attitude."

~Thomas Jefferson

Attitude has no gray area. Your attitude is either good or bad, right or wrong, positive or negative. There is a saying that a bad attitude is like a flat tire: you can't go anywhere until you change it.

It's easy to have a good attitude when everything is going well, but what happens when your life is in chaos and everything is out of control? In times of crisis, no right skills can take the place of the wrong attitude. As a matter of fact, good talent with bad attitude equals bad talent! A good look with a bad attitude makes one ugly.

Wrong attitude towards life is a choice that if left unchecked, limits the full capacity of the human potential.

Attitudes can change, not by accident or chance, but by habitual practice. You are responsible for changing your attitude. You must choose if you will be like a thermometer that reflects the attitudes of others around you, or if you will be the thermostat that sets and influences the attitudes of those around you. If I may emphasize this a different way, when it comes to developing a right attitude, each person is responsible for his or her attitude. You are not a passenger in a vehicle in which you hope the driver will get you to the right attitude; instead, you are the driver, the one who steers your life to or away from the right attitude.

Anyone can adopt a new attitude, but it must begin with repositioning the mind—a thought displacement. We must spend our creative energies in formulating ways and ideas how things can be accomplished, rather than exhaustively defending why they cannot be done. Too many people think of improvement or change as coming from the outside, but true change starts on the inside. Actions are important, but equally important is attitude. It is possible to be well-meaning and do the right thing with a wrong attitude. Attitude changes the whole experience.

"The most significant change in a person's life is a change in attitude. Right attitudes produce right actions."

~William J. Johnson

Ten Ways to Develop a Winning Attitude

Now that you know that your attitude is a choice you make, let's explore ways of developing those attitudes that push us toward greatness.

1. Time-Out Hurdle

Ask yourself this question: "Do I have a habit of taking time to reflect before responding?" If you're like most people, you respond spontaneously to challenges. You probably tend to deal with things emotionally and erratically, rather than rationally. Some of the best decisions are made in moments of reflecting and processing, rather than in flashes of reaction. The magnitude of the crisis should not dictate your reaction. You don't have to deal with everything right away. Sometimes, taking time to think over the situation and anticipate the different outcomes can help you form the correct response to what you are facing. Taking time out also helps consider multiple perspectives or approaches, even solutions, to the problem that you would otherwise not see in the heat of reacting.

2. Take Control of Your Response

In developing and building a winning attitude, you must simply learn to exert a greater sense of control over your environment and emotions, and to be objective in your response to each circumstance. If you believe a situation is temporary, your approach is different from a crisis you perceive as permanent. A sense of despair descends upon you by thinking that a single event is tied to your life forever and affects your destiny. By accepting this fatalistic mentality, you lose the courage to seek an alternate solution and to solve the problem of the moment. Learn to choose your response wisely and position yourself to determine your response, rather than react to the problem. Whenever you react to a problem, you relinquish your control over the circumstance, but whenever you respond, you maintain your control.

3. Isolate the Events and Compartmentalize Your Emotions

Do not allow one bad incident at the beginning of your day to disrupt the entire week or month and everything else that's happening in your life. Begin to see every challenge as specific and separate from other events of your life by putting things in their proper perspective. People with a bad attitude tend to exaggerate things and expand the scope of their problems; they want others to see just how problematic and disadvantaged their lives are. Do not be like this.

One door closing doesn't mean that you stop pursuing your dreams. You simply find another door. The pessimistic, superstitious mind believes one storm of life is a chain reaction, a consequence of something else they did or didn't do. They have not learned to disconnect the present challenge from other events occurring in their lives. Don't get bogged down by the details you are experiencing, because you will become easily overwhelmed then discouragement kicks in, which can quickly change your perspective of life.

Emotions at any given time have a significant influence on the outcome of your decisions. When emotions are high or low, they affect your perspective and decision-making process. By isolating life's events, and compartmentalizing your different emotions in these different circumstances, it allows you to remain objective, and you can focus on the main issue. It also helps us maintain emotional control and solve one problem at a time, live one day at a time, and keeps our eyes on the goal, instead of the distractions or the excitements. This eventually helps maintain a proper attitude, even when some things are not going your way.

Every day is a new day; every opportunity is another chance to move toward your best days.

4. Accept Challenges as Part of Life's Process

Ups and downs comprise life. Professional golfer Gary Player said, "To succeed in life, one must have determination and must be prepared to suffer during the process. If one isn't prepared to suffer during adversities, I don't really see how he can be successful." People with a winning attitude have problems just like everyone else; however, what distinguishes them from the masses is that they understand that storms, or sufferings, are a part of life. The key is to shift focus from the pain of the present to the joy of a desired future. Do not dwell on your pain too long, because it steals your joy; instead, redirect your focus to things and people that bring joy and fulfillment in your life.

When a woman gives birth to a baby, she accepts the some-times-unpleasant task of changing diapers and the responsibility of feeding the baby as part of the process of being a mother. Rather than complaining about the stinky diapers and the seemingly endless chores that come with raising children, this mother chooses to focus on the blessing of a child. She knows that she cannot enjoy the blessing of a newborn without embracing the possibility of the challenges. Every opportunity presented to you comes with possible challenges, so choose to see every challenge as an opportunity and part of a process.

5. *Stop Complaining*

Whenever you want to complain about your circumstance, there will always be something to complain about.

Never complain about what you are unwilling to change. Murmuring and complaining breed wrong attitudes. Some people complain about everything—where they were born, what they are dealing with, their hardships, their misfortune, the weather, the economy, their marriage, their children, the government, their income, their career... the list goes on and on. Complaining is talking negatively about things that are not necessarily wrong. When things are truly wrong, and you are expressing why they are wrong, you are simply expressing dissatisfaction. Complaining, on the other hand, is grumbling and whining about things we have done nothing to change or correct.

"Troubles, like babies, grow larger by nursing."

~Lady Holland

Think of a person complaining that he has only one pair of shoes. Then, consider the person who has no shoes. Imagine this person complaining about not having shoes, and then ponder a person who has no legs and no way to wear shoes. Complainers lack a proper perspective of life and what's important. Complaining only highlights your perception of the problem, but doesn't change it. It is an adult tantrum that raises awareness of dissatisfaction, yet doesn't provide a solution. When has your complaining about the weather ever changed it? When has your complaining about the government changed the way it operates? You have to stop complaining and take action to correct the problem. In the words of Orin Woodward: "Leaders identify what's wrong, so they can fix it; others identify what's wrong, so they can complain."

6. Help Other People

One of the easiest ways to fix a bad attitude is to help other people. When you are not so self-consumed, but instead care about, even help, others, it makes a huge difference in your attitude. When you impact the lives of others besides yourself, you build a sense of significance and value.

Sometimes by helping others, you actually help yourself. Zig Ziglar said that we can get anywhere we want to go by helping others get where they want to go. I have had friends who did mission work in other countries, and one thing they all shared upon returning to their native countries was a new perception of life and the discovery of how blessed and privileged they were in comparison with other people. Some were forever challenged, and their outlook of life had been completely transformed.

"If you are all wrapped up in yourself, you're overdressed."

~Kate Halverson

7. *Choose an Attitude of Gratitude and Expectation*

If there is one principle that I can say has had a significant impact in my life it is being grateful for what I have at every present moment. Charles Swindoll said, "We cannot change our past. We cannot change the fact that people act in a certain way. We cannot change the inevitable. The only thing we can do is play on the one string we have, and that is our attitude." A right attitude doesn't come from being a moral person or a religious person. Attitude is a choice. Regardless of whether you are a morning person or not, when your feet hit the floor, you must decide to wake up happy, sing in the shower, wake up to music, listen to inspirational message, use positive self-talk, and choose to be optimistic. It's hard to change your attitude without changing your self-talk.

Decide and choose the aggregate of our attitudes in response to critical issues at every time. This, in return, provides a systematic, yet practical, method of predetermining what we will do in different situations. For instance, raising the bar on what makes us angry and not allowing someone's pettiness or immaturity to bring out the worst in us. Chris Widener, a speaker and author said, "Instead of spending your time thinking about how bad things are, think about how good they will be." When we choose an attitude of gratitude, we give ourselves permission to expect the best.

"The last of the human freedoms is to choose one's attitudes."

~Viktor Frankl

8. Don't Take Failure Personally

Your life is too complex to be defined by a single short-coming in your life.

Success in life is less influenced by the struggles you face, but more importantly by your outlook. You cannot take one incident of failure and allow it to drag you down. If you want to be positive, celebrate the lessons learned through your failures. It's up to you to change how you interpret past failures: as lessons or as learning experiences. Everyone fails at some point in life. You cannot always win, but you must always learn from your failures in order to win. Learn to redefine failures as a learning experience, not a permanent event. People with a winning attitude see failure as external, as if something outside of their control caused the event; whereas, losers process failure as internal. They tend to see failure as a pervasive occurrence or a lifelong epidemic in their lives, which they use to justify their bad attitudes.

"What is the difference between an obstacle and adversity? Your Attitude."

~J. Sidlow Baxter

9. Be Content at Different Stages of Life

When you develop a spirit of contentment, you learn to appre-ciate, and are satisfied with, God's sufficient provisions, which you currently enjoy. Whenever you are ungrateful of what you have, you fail to understand, or see, that even that can be taken away. As pastor and author James MacDonald puts it, "Contentment is a settled sense of adequacy." When you learn to be content at different stages of life, you develop a positive attitude toward life—an attitude of gratitude.

Having more possessions doesn't equate to a happier life, and having less is not the key to godliness. Make up your mind to be happy and content in whatever circumstance you are in. When you are content, your attitude is of joy and satisfaction, and you develop an ability to enjoy the ordinary moments of life, such as a caring conversation with loved ones, a moment of relaxation and reflection, while enjoying the beauty of nature, instead of rushing to the next urgent matter.

In the Bible, Paul wrote, "Not that I speak in regard to need, for I have learned in whatever state I am, to be content."[4] Contentment doesn't mean that your life is perfect, but it's peaceful because you are enjoying the sufficiency of the moment and not being pressured by the cares to acquire more through greed.

10. Learn to Deal with Frustrations and Rejection

The path to greatness is filled with many variables, including moments of frustrations and rejection. Your response matters. Most, if not all, of the world's great people have encountered and dealt with their share of life's frustrations. When you don't learn how to process and deal with the frustrations that come into your life, you end up projecting those frustrations to everyone around you. To be great, learn how to deal with life's frustrations.

When you encounter rejection, don't fall into the trap of developing a bad attitude by thinking that rejection is personal. For every *yes* you seek, you will have a categorical *no*. But, always remember that for every *no* you receive, you will be a step closer to receiving the right *yes*. Some of the most celebrated, uncommon achievers were rejected many times. Abraham Lincoln was one of America's greatest presidents. He is a strong example of learning to deal with frustrations and rejection, while maintaining a great attitude. He didn't have a few frustrations in his life; rather, he had several, many of which you and I may never have to face. He had a nervous breakdown and was bedridden for six months. He ran for Congress and lost the race four times. His fiancée died days before their wedding. He failed in business, but still had a great attitude of success.

It is paramount in maintaining a courageous attitude that you understand that denial doesn't constitute rejection, but direction. Take every categorical *no* you receive as a motivation to move closer to the *yes* you are pursuing. It is in developing a good self-image, regardless of those who deny you that you gain the courage to move beyond rejection. Leaders have learned how to turn rejection into positive energy, while others turn rejection into permanent excuses.

PHINEHAS'S AXIOMS

- Unless you deal with what's in you, you will blame the world around you, while the real issue is your attitude.
- Nothing is as powerful as attitude in shaping your character and developing your ability to pursue and reach your potential.
- High achievers and consistently motivated people are always people with a great attitude.
- Attitude dictates your response to the present and shapes your expectation of the future.
- It is not so much skill that determines one's ability to climb the highest mountain; rather, it's one's attitude to overcome all obstacles and scale the mountain.
- A leader's performance and success are influenced greatly by his or her attitude—even more than his or her attributes.
- You are incapable of manifesting your full, unlimited potential without a great positive attitude toward life.
- Learn to reframe past negative experiences into a catalyst for personal advancement.
- You will always underperform when you feel incapable. Self-concepts affect self-conduct.
- What you believe of yourself might not be true, yet your environment will influence your beliefs and reinforce your attitudes, be they right or wrong.
- Your outlook of life is contaminated by the toxicity of your inner thoughts.

- Personal appearance always affects your attitude, as well as your performance.
- It's never about your present trials; it's always about your future triumphs.
- Your attitude is the weather forecast that predicts how your day will look like; make it a brighter day.
- In times of crisis, no right skills can take the place of the wrong attitude.
- Wrong attitude toward life is a choice that if left unchecked, limits the full capacity of the human potential.
- Every day is a new day; every opportunity is another chance to move toward your best days.
- Some of the best decisions are made in moments of reflecting and processing, rather than in flashes of reaction.
- Whenever you want to complain about your circumstance, there will always be something to complain about.
- Your life is too complex to be defined by a single shortcoming in your life.
- It is paramount in maintaining a courageous attitude that denial doesn't constitute rejection, but direction.

3

CHOOSE TO THINK DIFFERENTLY

"The significant problems we have cannot be solved at the same level of thinking with which we created them."

~Albert Einstein

It seems obvious to discuss the topic of thinking, because living requires thinking. Like many other behaviors, thinking correctly and critically matters, and it's something that does not come automatically; rather, it must be learned. Becoming a better thinker requires creating the right conditions and environment that will foster great thinking. Many people have become victims of the desensitization and *dumbing down* of society through television, video games, tabloids, social media, and meaningless reality shows. Most people today prefer not to have to think too much, which only reaffirms the words of Martin Luther King Jr.: "Rarely do we find men who willingly engage in hard solid thinking. There is almost universal quest for easy answers and half-baked solutions. Nothing pains some people more than having to think."

To maximize your potential and attain personal greatness, you must begin with an investment in your capacity to think. Your level of living is the direct result of your level of thinking.

No matter the profession, the ability to think is always needed. It is hard to overstate the value of not only thinking, but also thinking differently. It is impossible to reach your ultimate potential and realize your full capacity without developing the ability not only to think independently, but also to think correctly. Many people are held back from attaining their potential, because they fail to understand the value of investing in their capacity for good thinking.

Thinking affects feelings. It also affects actions; therefore, it affects everything you do. If thinking affects behavior, then taking charge of your thoughts will influence your feelings, which in turn will influence behavior and affect your actions, eventually leading to a different and more desired outcome.

Great thinking unlocks human potential and accelerates personal achievement.

"Thinking provides you with a practical step by step guide that empowers leaders of all abilities and degrees to realize their greatest potential."[1] What vastly distinguishes human beings from animals is our capacity for logical thinking and innovation, and no matter how technologically advanced humans become, we will always need to exploit our capacity to think. Thinking is a part of everyone's life, yet not everyone seems to practice great thinking. As a matter of fact, your creative capacity to think needs to increase to keep pace with the complexity of the technologically advanced world we live in.

You may have dreams, ideas, and innovative thoughts, but be diligent not to fall into the trap of envisioning these new ideas as only pie in the sky; rather, engage wholeheartedly by actively pursuing and achieving these dreams. Learn how to convert your thoughts from concept to reality and our dreams from mere dreaming to becoming, as I discuss in depth in my previous book, *From Dreaming to Becoming.*[2]

Great thinkers not only think on a consistent basis, but also create ideas that solve problems and advance humanity.

Too many people are stuck in their present state and have failed to entertain thoughts of seizing their future. Life has conditioned them to think of taking care of only the present—paying bills and making a living—but they are not engaged in great thinking, which would help them find solutions as to how to alter their present and create the future they desire. Greatness demands that we create the new reality we envision and not remain fixated on only maintaining our present conditions. If you desire to improve your circumstances, you must first improve your thoughts and learn how to think differently, which is not automatic as most people assume. Thinking differently can be difficult, but the more you practice good thinking, the more you develop capacity for great thinking.

You cannot produce high-level results with sub-standard thinking. Your life will conform to the pattern of your thoughts. Think big and flood your mind with uncommon ideas, creative thoughts, and great imaginations that will give birth to great possibilities. Develop the ability to cultivate a new paradigm that elevates you from mediocrity to greatness. Nothing will change in your life if you don't first change your thinking. Personal greatness is built on the foundation of new thoughts. In the words of James Allen, "Man is made or unmade by himself. In the memory of thought, he forges the weapons by which he destroys himself. He also fashions the tools with which he builds for himself heavenly mansions of joy and strength and peace."[3]

Superior thoughts will not develop from shallow minds.

It is imperative that you invest in your mind. In the words of Author Napoleon Hill, "More gold has been mined from thoughts of man than has ever been taken from the earth." Our minds are the warehouse of great thoughts and ideas. In studying the behavior and beliefs of successful people, I have observed a common thread in their underlying perception regarding life. It asserts that one's quality of life is proportionate to one's state of mind. Here are a few remarkable statements that affirm this truth:

- "The greatest discovery of our time is that human beings, by changing their inner attitude of their heart, ultimately change the outer aspect of their lives." *Sir Williams James*
- "A man is literary what he thinks, his character being the complete sum of all his thoughts." *James Allen*
- "Nurture your mind with great thoughts, for you will never go any higher than you think." *Benjamin Disraeli*
- "The man who acquires the ability to take full possession of his own mind may take possession of anything else, which he is justly entitled." *Andrew Carnegie*
- "As a man thinks in his heart so is he." *Proverbs 23:7a*

Thinking Differently

To think like successful people, you must cultivate the practice of seeing things differently.

You might wonder what makes the top world-class achievers attain significant success. While several factors or skills contribute, the most dominant reason is their capacity to think differently than the average person. John Maxwell posits that "Unsuccessful people focus on thinking on survival; average people focus their thinking on maintenance; and successful people focus their thinking on progress."[4]

"The real voyage of discovery lies not in seeking new landscapes, but in seeing with new eyes."

~Marcel Proust

One of the greatest impediments of seeing with new eyes and thereby thinking in terms of success is old patterns of thought. This wrong and erroneous old pattern of thoughts persisted over time becomes our core conviction. This core conviction shapes our perceptions. Your perception causes you to see life from a certain lens or set of rules that you assume to be true and important to you, even though they could be erroneous. It is said that whatever you label a thing, that is what it becomes to you; your perception becomes your reality.

This set of assumptions or rules ends up controlling how we see things and to some major extent affects the decisions we make and how we respond to new information. These rules become the playbook rules that control everything you do. Therefore, in-order to think differently and achieve your dreams, it will be imperative to change your perception first before you attempt to change the quality of your life. This can only be effective if you begin with changing your paradigm, since your paradigm controls your perception. The truth is the distance between your present reality and the manifestation of your desired dream will be determined by how fast you are willing to change your existing paradigm. You must actively and purposely force your brain out of routine and predictable perceptions and into perceiving things you've never seen before.

The distance between your present reality and the manifestation of your desired dream will be determined by how fast you are willing to change your existing paradigm.

To think differently, you must commit to lifelong learning by exposing your mind to new stimuli. Gregory Berns explains in his book *Iconoclast* that "Iconoclast [is] a person who is able to do things that others say it can't be done because an iconoclast perceives things different than other people. To see things differently than other people the most effective solution is to bombard the brain with things it has never encountered before. Novelty releases the perceptual process from the shackles of past experiences and forces the brain to make new judgments."[5]

"Conceptually, stuck systems cannot become unstuck simply by trying harder. For a fundamental reorientation to occur, that spirit

of adventure which optimizes serendipity, and which enables new perceptions beyond the control of our thinking processes must happen first."

~Ed Friedman

Most times, our perception is built from how we interpret things based on personal belief. This perception then becomes our reality from which we draw conclusions and judgments. It is said that we don't see life as it is, but as we are. Certain factors predispose our brains to certain default mechanisms and establish our belief system from which we see life. These factors distort our perception and results, giving us skewed interpretations and responses, influenced by the negative experiences in our lives. Many sources have contributed to this skewed interpretation and influenced our perception:

Environment—neighborhoods, social exposure, people or places, upbringing

Associations—authority figures, family members, teachers, relatives, institutions

Repetitive Information—learned behavior that forms our belief system, which determines our actions

Habits—patterns that have positively or negatively conditioned our thinking

Personal Experience—past encounters, fears, desires, consequences

In her book *Mindset*, Stanford University psychologist, Carol S. Dweck discovered during her twenty years of research that "the view that one adopts for their lives, profoundly affects the way they lead their lives. It can determine whether one becomes the person they want to be and accomplish the things they value."[6] In other words, the outcome of our lives is directly correlated with our outlook. Your self-perception is therefore the foundation upon which your life is built. Every aspect of your life, such as the way you feel about yourself, the quality of your relationships, the career you pursue, or the goals and dreams you accomplish, will significantly be impacted by your thoughts.

The Two Mindsets

Dr. Dweck further explains in her book that in learning to fulfill our potential and increasing our capacity, we must explore two fundamental beliefs: a *fixed mindset* and a *growth mindset*. The fixed mindset is based on a belief that one's qualities are carved in stone and that each individual has a certain amount of intelligence, a certain personality, and a certain moral character. She says that this mindset is based on the concept that each one of us has to play the game of life with the hand we were dealt and that we are expected to accept our lives as it is, because that's apparently what life has offered us. So, we live life trying to convince ourselves and others that we are holding a royal flush, while secretly worrying that it is really only a pair of tens. People with a fixed mindset do not take charge of their abilities or motivation. They are insecure and highly sensitive about being wrong or making mistakes. They tend to prove themselves over and over again, because they don't want to look deficient in any way.

The second mindset according to her research is a growth mindset, which is based on a belief that one's basic qualities can be cultivated through effort. Despite the differences that may initially exist in one's talents and aptitudes, interests and temperaments, everyone can change and grow through application and experience. When someone has a growth mindset, he or she focuses on self-development, self-motivation, and personal responsibility. People with a growth mindset are oriented toward learning and improving, and not just winning. They thrive in challenges because challenges make them stretch and develop their potential. We can therefore assume that to attain our maximum capacity, we must think differently—to overcome a fixed mindset and adopt a growth mindset that forces our brains to think in a new paradigm.

"Everyone thinks of changing the world, but no one thinks of changing himself."

~Leo Tolstoy

How to Develop Good Thinking

Given this new understanding, you have to cultivate the practice of thinking differently. But this presents a question: How do we develop our ability to good thinking? In his book *Thinking for a Change*, John Maxwell shares six steps in the process of how to become a good thinker.[7]

1. Expose Yourself to Good Input

You are capable of good thinking, but you must expose yourself first to good input that would stir up your mind and provoke great thinking. You must be able to identify and explore good input. This can be accomplished by the books, magazines, and blogs you read or listen to. I enjoy listening to podcasts and audio books, and I watch YouTube videos, such as the Ted Talks, to stimulate my thinking. Visit new places, meet new people, and learn new skills. Great thoughts can come from anywhere at any given time. Mark Twain said, "Travel is fatal to prejudice, bigotry and narrow mindedness, and many of our people need it sorely on these accounts. Broad, wholesome, charitable view of men and things cannot be acquired by vegetating in one little corner of the earth all of one's lifetime." Get a portfolio and develop the practice of saving in it creative ideas that inspire you. Or start a journal of thoughts, sayings, or other inspirations, and revisit and revise it as needed, thereby stimulating your thoughts with creative ideas and insights that lead to good thinking.

2. Expose Yourself to Good Thinkers

Spending time with great thinkers will increase your capacity for good thinking. Interactions with people of diverse viewpoints expose you to new ideas. A Bible proverb states, *"Keep company with the wise and you will become wise. If you make friends with stupid people, you will be ruined."*[8] Your circle of influence should include great thinkers who can challenge your thoughts. You can grow your thinking in a linear way through experience, but you can also grow your thinking exponentially through engagement with other great thinkers. I believe that if you are the smartest in your group of thinkers, you are in the wrong group.

It's easier to gain a lot more perspective from other people's thoughts than to develop the thoughts by yourself.

3. Choose to Think Good Thoughts

Thinking is a discipline, so make a habit of being intentional in capturing good thoughts. We live in a negative world, and most of the news is negative; therefore, set a time and a place to engage with good thoughts and ideas. Good thoughts give birth to more good thoughts and ideas. The more you think good thoughts, the more good thoughts come to you. Paraphrasing the words of Paul the apostle, "Whatever things are true, whatever things are noble, whatever things are just, whatever things pure, whatever things lovely, and whatever things of good report ... meditate on these things."[9]

What you perpetually think about determines what you pursue. So, create a data bank of good thoughts and ultimately, your life will change correspondingly.

4. Act on Your Good Thoughts

In the words of Napoleon Hill, "Action is the real measure of intelligence." Don't just think good thoughts, but also follow through to put your thoughts into action. Thoughts precede action. Good thinking needs to be transformed into action. Great thoughts without action are as detrimental as bad thoughts with action. Making excuses instead of taking massive action to pursue your thoughts only creates added obstacles and reasons why you can't actualize these thoughts. In the words of Claude M. Bistol, author of *The Magic of Believing*, "The successful people in industry have succeeded through their thinking. Their hands were helpers to their brains." Thoughts alone without action never generate results, so practice acting on your good thoughts.

5. Allow Your Emotions to Create Another Good Thought

Your past hurts and negative experiences can prevent you from spending productive time thinking, because of the emotions and feelings you developed from them. It is at that moment when your emotions are low and perhaps a demand is made on you to create a good thought that you are least likely and incapable of creating a good thought. Those who engage in good thinking use their emotions to create a mental momentum, but they determine not to rely on their feelings to think. So, regardless of how you feel and how your emotions are in any given moment, you cannot rely on your emotions, or even allow these negative feelings, to deter you from creating good thoughts. Instead, use the feelings to propel you and give you mental momentum and energy to create more good thoughts.

Our capacity for great thinking can be deterred or advanced by our current emotions.

6. Repeat the Process

Keep growing and improving by reading and thinking, then repeat these steps of good thinking. What you repetitively do and practice, you will eventually master.

3 Ways to Start Thinking Differently

"The difficulty lays not so much in developing new ideas as in escaping from old ones."

~John Maynard Keynes

Think beyond the norm. Most people never venture to think beyond the initial ideas they have. They fail to explore the greater possibilities that remain beneath the initial thought.

1. Practice Non-Conformity Thinking
"Conformity is the jailer of freedom and the enemy of growth."

~John F. Kennedy

Most people stick with status quo thinking, because they want to blend in with the crowd and not stand out. True mavericks don't follow the rules; they break them. As young children, we were taught to color within the lines, to put round pegs into round holes, to blend in with the world around us—all of which limited our creative capacity. Those who failed to adhere to the way things were "meant to be" were labeled as renegades or misfits, but those who conformed to the norm were rewarded with distinction and honors.

We went to school and learned from a curriculum that someone who didn't know us had developed years before. By the time the curriculum arrived in our classrooms, it was becoming obsolete and was not adapted to a fast-paced evolving global market or to technological advances. This kind of limiting mindset and beliefs exists in people like Charles H. Duell, the director of the U.S. Patent Office in 1899, who said, "Everything that can be invented has been invented." A century later, we see how wrong he was. Imagine if we all ascribed to this short-sighted, and mistaken, thinking; we could have hindered ourselves and the human race from reaching the accomplishments we have experienced so far. Our education might train us what to think, but it may never show us how to think and ways of thinking correctly.

Society has set limitations on our creative capacity through common conventional linear thinking.

Steve Jobs once observed the following:

"When you grow up you tend to get told that the world is the way it is and your life is just to live your life inside the world. Try not to bash into the walls too much. Try to have a nice family life, have fun, save a little money. That's a very limited life. Life can be much broader once you discover one simple fact: Everything around you that you call life was made up by people that were no smarter than you. And you can change it, you can influence it… Once you learn that, you'll never be the same again."[10]

At the turn of the twentieth century, Henry Ford developed the process of mass production in manufacturing the Model T automobile. The assembly line set the standard for industrial production and became the prominent form of manufacturing. The process used on a moving belt assembly line where each section of the automobile manufacture was broken down into small parts. As components moved down the assembly line, workers fitted the parts into the automobile, until it was completed. This simplified process required unskilled and uneducated workers. The end result was routine tasks that limited people's creative capacity. In essence, people became mechanical robots. Today, multiple industries use this process.

"If everyone is thinking alike somebody isn't thinking."
~George S. Patton

Several years ago, I worked for a customer service center. I was given a script I was to follow verbatim, and the quality control department assessed me as to how well I followed the script. It got so imprinted in my mind that after all these years; I can still recite the script. Granted, the goal was brand consistency and quality, as well as predictable service; however, the end result was a work-force who would not think independently. In the words of Jack Welch, former CEO of General Electric, "Ninety-nine point nine percent of all employees are in the pile because they don't think."

In order to reach your ultimate potential, you have to push beyond the limiting factors of conformity linear thinking and choose to think differently by engaging in non-conformity exponential thinking.

Conformity linear thinking is automated response thinking, status quo thinking, and a routine programming that requires no effort or creativity— similar to the assembly line model in which one follows the steps over and over and *over* again. This is think-ing as everyone would have you think; it's textbook thinking, it's thinking per the expectation of society that attempts to force everyone into a mold. It kills our creative capacity.

Non-conformity exponential thinking is creative thinking that overcomes popular thinking. This kind of thinking is non-habitual, relies on multiple disciplines, and explores multiple seemingly unrelated fields, yet has a common thread or similar elements combining to form an entirely new way of thinking and doing.

Some people might believe that they are not artistic or creative enough to come up with great thoughts—thoughts outside of the norm. But, creative thoughts don't have to necessarily be original thoughts. We can establish a thought pattern that originates from seemingly unrelated fields, yet gives us new perceptive or a new approach to an existing problem. Daniel Pink observes in his book, *A Whole New Mind*, "What's the greatest demand today isn't analysis but synthesis [the ability to put together the pieces] seeing the big picture, crossing boundaries, and being able to combine disparate pieces into an arresting new whole."[11]

The world today has changed tremendously in just the past twenty years, and with accessibility to the Internet, educational resources, encyclopedias, journals, magazines, research papers, and sites like YouTube, your creative ability can be awakened by looking for innovative ideas that provoke your mind to think differently. In becoming a great thinker, your ability to detect coexisting relationships in apparent independent ideas or concepts will make you more creative in piecing the whole together.

Henry David Thoreau wrote, "Many an object is not seen, though it falls within the range of our visual ray, because it does not come within the range of our intellectual ray."

The following chart helps us to see the difference between strategic or non-conformity thinkers and conformity or conventional thinkers.[12]

Strategic thinkers are . . .	Conventional thinkers are . . .
Future-based: They anticipate change and look for opportunities that may arise.	**Reactive:** They rarely initiate ideas and wait to be told what to do or what actions to take.
Curious: They are interested in what is going on throughout their department, organization, industry, and the larger business environment.	**Isolated:** They typically work without input from others or without understanding others' goals and objectives.
Long-term focus: They are willing to invest today to gain a better outcome tomorrow.	**Short-term focus:** They often do not consider the potential impact of an action on long-term goals.
Able to prioritize: They do not equate being busy with being effective. They place a high value on projects with the potential for great impact and return.	**Unable to prioritize:** They often treat all tasks equally without regard to impact.
Nimble: They are able to adjust and modify their approaches.	**Inflexible:** They may be unwilling to alter their plans even when adjustments could yield a better return.
Life-long learner: They proac-	**Satisfied:** They normally are not

tively seek knowledge and skills and are willing to teach others.	interested in learning new things or methods and are content with their current capabilities.
Creative: They consider unorthodox ideas.	**Predictable:** They often stick with familiar paths.

1. Engage in Possibility Thinking

When it comes to thinking, choose thoughts that lead to the best possible solutions, regardless of anticipated resistance. You have to push beyond the limits, beyond every perceived limitation—most people stop thinking of possibilities the moment an objection arises. Success will come from challenging what you or others have already accomplished and not settling where others who preceded you reached. There is always a better way. To step into greatness, you must seek for ways to improve or uncomplicate whatever solution you seek to offer.

Possibility thinking awakens your imagination, and imagination births your creative capacity, which unlocks your unlimited potential.

Get outside of yourself, your little world, and your own interests and start looking at life and the world around you from a different perspective. Stop exploring possibilities and opportunities pessimistically, trying to assess why it wouldn't work, and instead embrace a possibility mentality why it would work. What other possibilities are there? What are others missing to see that you have the capacity to see into and improve on?

We can all benefit from adopting new ideas or expanding on existing ideas. Sometimes, it's not about reinventing the wheel, but refining or modifying a part of the wheel. I know a man who is building and testing a flying car, a concept that takes an already existing product that most of us own and improves on it, so he can help others realize the dream of a flying car.

You don't need to have a formal education to think differently; neither do you need to be an insider or an expert in an industry to revolutionize the industry. You only need a capacity to think differently. You also don't have to always think up something new or come up with something that does not exist. You can work with a simple and basic existing product and add a wow factor to embellish it. Consider something you use every day that could be improved upon. What can you develop or improve on in order to create a better, easier, more efficient, and profitable product?

Sometimes, it's all about improving a process or a service. Uber's premise was to revolutionize the taxi transport industry. They never invented the car, built an infrastructure, or hired employees. They improved a service. Netflix did not invent DVD movie rentals; they improved a process. Blockbuster had dominated the DVD rental market (and generated a large percentage of its revenue from penalizing its users with late fees). Netflix established a simple fee structure that did not burden users with late fees; neither did they open brick-and-mortar stores. They simply shipped their movies from multiple regional warehouses, and customers had the freedom to keep the DVD as long as they wanted without a late fee. They also introduced a streaming service, making a number of their movies instantly available at minimal cost. This revolutionized the DVD rental industry and put Blockbuster out of business.

Possibility thinking gives birth to more possibilities. In the words of William Arthur Ward, "Nothing limits achievement like small thinking; nothing expands possibilities like unleashed thinking." Think broadly, as Judge Oliver Wendell Holmes, Jr. stated, "A mind that is stretched by a new experience can never go back to its old dimension."

Have you exploited the full capability of your potential? Is it possible that there could be more than your eye can see right now? What new seas of invention have you not charted?

"You see things; and say "why?" But I dream things that never were; and I say "why not?"

~George Bernard Shaw

2. Develop Collaborative Thinking

"Great thoughts that come with concentration can often be enhanced through collaboration."

~Brian Dodd

John Maxwell says, "We tend to think of great thinkers and innovators as soloists, but the truth is that the greatest innovative thinking doesn't occur in a vacuum."[13] Teams win games and championships, not individuals. Ken Blanchard said, "None of us is as smart as all of us." We learn faster when we enlist the help of others.

I have observed that great ideas emerge from collaborative thinking, and full participation of others help us sort through both good ideas and bad ideas, enabling us to refine our good ideas and develop them into great ideas.

Greatness is never achieved alone, but through collaboration with others.

"We are now entering a "mind-share" world, no longer just dealing with analytic and procedural problems that require rational solutions. We're being asked to think together in ways that are innovative and relational. People who never met are being forced to come up with breakthrough solutions. We're being asked to think together in ways that are innovative and relational. People who have never met are being forced to come up with breakthrough solutions to complex problems. We must work and think across continents, cultures, time zones and temperatures."[14]

"Each mind has its own method."
~Ralph Waldo Emerson

How can we think with others across continents, cultures, time zones, and temperatures, while effectively consolidating our thinking, so as to leverage our collaborative thinking? In their book *Collaborative Intelligence*, [15] Markova and McArthur state that there are differences in how we think, so we have to learn to acknowledge and recognize the differences. They refer to this ability as Collaborative Intelligence Quotient (CQ), which is the measure of one's ability to think with those who think differently on what matters to us all. They came up with a system to help us understand the different patterns of thinking, learning, and com-municating "mind-patterns," which help to recognize the unique and specific ways individuals' process information. Understanding how differently each of us think will help us bridge the variations between us and others and also foster effective communication, so that we can decipher and understand the mind-patterns of those with whom we are engaging in collaborative thinking.

The authors assert that to recognize mind-patterns, we have to start with attention. Attention regulates our flow of information, which is how we process information and what we notice in every-thing we encounter. According to the authors, attention is divided into three states: *focused attention, sorting attention,* and *open attention*. Our minds constantly and quickly shift between these three states of attention at any given moment as we are thinking.

Focused attention is a conscious state of mind in which thoughts become certain and form into solid beliefs. At this stage of thinking, someone is usually directed and concentrates on what is in front of him or her. This state of attention is suited for concentrating on accomplishing tasks, making decisions, or attending to details and timelines.

Sorting attention describes a subconscious state in which thoughts wander back and forth, sorting through information and comparing one thing to another. This is suited for trying to understand, digesting information or experiences, thinking through confusion, or weighing through multiple choices.

The third state is what Markova and McArthur call *open attention*, the unconscious state of mind in which thoughts are very wide and internal. This third state is for imagining possibilities, creative thoughts, and daydreams. This is the state in which we get in touch with memories, images, and ideas, then transform them into new patterns—new ways to approach old problems, exploring different options by seeing situations or problems in new ways, and associating past experiences, stories, and people.

When we are thinking, our minds naturally shift from one state of attention to another, taking in new information—organizing it, digesting it, evaluating it, discarding it, or arranging it into new patterns and ideas; then finally sorting it, storing it, and deciding how to express it. So, in thinking with others, we have to understand that people, at any given time, are in different states of thinking and different ways of paying attention. Whether someone is exploring, wondering, imagining, reflecting, or sorting, these are all different stages of effective thinking. The mistaken assumption is that only focused attention is valuable, so when someone is confused while sorting information, we think they need assistance, because we feel they ought to take swift action and decide something now. But, in understanding the three states of attention, we know this assumption is not true.

Effective collaborative thinking demands that we must be willing to spend time not knowing the immediate solution to the objective at hand; instead, we have to engage with the mind wide open and think with others differently. It means that we learn to value the thoughts of others without dictating their process of thought. To experience collaborative thinking, we must align ourselves with people of diverse opinions, but similar objectives, people who will temporarily sacrifice their uniqueness and perspective for the greater good—for achieving the common goal. Effective collaborative thinking will occur when we build a team of people whose input creates new ideas of highest value, people who are not narcissistic, but who cooperate and complement others' ideas, people secure in their gifts and abilities and willing to embrace others' ideas, while not shying away from contributing their thoughts and ideas, as well. Collaborative thinkers celebrate diversity as a strength, not a threat.

Granted, to achieve your full potential, you must participate with others by engaging others' points of view, which in turn helps you to enlarge your view, your understanding, and your thinking through their feedback. Collaborative thinking allows you to share your platform with others who have similar thoughts to contribute their invaluable ideas.

If you want to think slowly, think alone; but if you want to think innovatively fast, think with others.

PHINEHAS'S AXIOMS

- To maximize your potential and attain personal greatness, begin with an investment in your capacity to think. Your level of living is the direct result of your level of thinking.

- Great thinking unlocks human potential and accelerates personal achievement.

- You cannot produce high-level results with sub-standard thinking.

- Personal greatness is built on the foundation of new thoughts.

- Great thinkers not only think on a consistent basis, but also create ideas that solve problems and advance humanity.

- Greatness demands that you create the new reality you envision, and not remain fixated on only maintaining your present conditions.

- One of the greatest impediments of seeing with new eyes and thereby thinking in terms of success is old patterns of thought.

- To think like successful people, cultivate the practice of seeing things differently.

- The distance between your present reality and the manifestation of your desired dream will be determined by how fast you are willing to change your existing paradigm.

- You must actively and purposely force your brain out of routine and predictable perceptions and into perceiving things you've never seen before.

- In other words, the outcome of your life is directly correlated with your outlook. Your self-perception is therefore the foundation upon which your life is built.
- It's easier to gain a lot more perspective from other people's thoughts, than to develop the thoughts by yourself.
- What you perpetually think about determines what you pursue. So, create a data bank of good thoughts, and ultimately your life will change correspondingly.
- Your capacity for great thinking can be deterred or advanced by your current emotions.
- Society has set limitations on your creative capacity through common conventional linear thinking.
- To reach your ultimate potential, you have to push beyond the limiting factors of conformity linear thinking and choose to see things differently by engaging in non-conformity exponential thinking.
- In becoming a great thinker, your ability to detect coexisting relationships in apparent independent ideas or concepts will make you more creative in piecing the whole together.
- Possibility thinking awakens your imagination, and imagination births your creative capacity, which unlocks your unlimited potential.
- Sometimes, it's not about reinventing the wheel, but refining or modifying a part of the wheel.
- Value the thoughts of others without dictating their process of thought.

- Greatness is never achieved alone, but through collaboration with others.
- Collaborative thinkers celebrate diversity as a strength, not a threat.
- If you want to think slowly, think alone; but if you want to think innovatively fast, think with others.

4

EMBRACE CHANGE AS AN ALLY

"For many people, change is more threatening than challenging. They see it as the destroyer of what is familiar and comfortable rather than the creator of what is new and exciting."

~Nido Qubein

The eagle is a fascinating and intelligent creature. Humans can learn from the eagles and how they initiate and manage change. Unlike most birds, eagles don't lay their eggs in a tree nest. Instead, it pitches the nest very high at the top of a cliff, away from predators. The male eagle gathers twigs to strategically weave the nest. Then, he places thorns on top of the twigs, after which he covers the thorns with soft grass. Finally, after several layers of thorns and grass, he plucks his feathers and lays them at the center of the nest, where the female eagle lays the eggs.

The male and female care for the eaglets, until it's time for them to learn how to fly. The female eagle throws the little eaglets outside the nest, but they jump back into the comfortable nest. The next time the mother eagle pushes the eaglets out of the nest, she removes the soft layers, leaving the thorns bare and exposed. When the scared eaglet jumps back into the nest, the thorns prick it. This discomfort forces the eaglet to jump back out of the nest. Next time around, the mother eagle pushes the little eaglet of the cliff as though by accident, yet it is by design. The scared eaglet plummets through the air in imminent danger of death and uncertain of what to do. Then, the male eagle swoops down, snatches the eaglet, and brings it back to the cliff. This scenario continues until eventually, the eaglet discovers that it is equipped with uncommon potential and capacity to fly. It spreads and flaps its little wings. Finally, the eaglet abdicates the comfort of the nest and the discomfort of the process and soars on its own. Until a bird flies away from its nest, only then will it discover that the world is bigger than the nest it was hatched in.

If you desire to reach your ultimate potential, you must disrupt the status quo and break the nest of your comfort.

One of the most indomitable forces on earth is change. Change creates events and forces us to make decisions we would otherwise not initiate on our own. Change happens with or without our acknowledgment or approval. Change is always inevitable and, in most cases, unprecedented. When change happens, it might bring either good or bad things, depending on our response towards the change.

Human beings are inclined to comfort; we sometimes fight to keep things as they have always been. Both organizations and individuals alike are creatures of routine. We like to be static because it makes us feel safe, as opposed to the dynamics and uncertainty of change. It is impossible to reach your highest potential, to be the best you, and move from obscurity to significance and greatness, without embracing change.

Most people are reluctant to change their habits; some refuse to change their belief systems or thoughts, their customs and traditions, or practices. Organizations that refuse change prefer to remain stuck in a plateau, rather than embrace transformation.

You've heard statements like, "If it's not broke, don't fix it" and "Better the devil you know than the angel you don't know," or perhaps you have heard the German proverb "An old error is more popular than a new truth." Those who hold to such premises maintain that they are safer by not trying new things, or new ways.

Most inventions were the result of someone challenging the status quo; people who believed in the premise that if it's not broke you need to break it. Sometimes, people stumbled onto innovations when the expected result failed, creating a new and better outcome.

These people were brave to defy the prevailing wisdom, thus giving birth to creative ideas.

Newton's first law of motion states that an object at rest stays at rest and an object in motion stays in motion with the same speed and in the same direction, unless acted on by an external force. It is the external forces of life—crises and challenges—that sometimes initiate change in our lives or our organizations. It's impossible to reach your ultimate human potential without embracing the concept of change, just as without change, the beauty of butterflies would be nonexistent.

To be great, you not only have to embrace and desire change, but you must also learn how to navigate through change itself.

Break the Nest

Most people and organizations remain sequestered in the comfort of their environments so long that they fail to discover their wings. Just like the mother eagle disrupts the eaglets, along come outside forces that compel us to do something new if we want to soar. These situations induce a sense of urgency that challenges our comfort zones. It means removing the sources of comfort, the "soft layers" that make us complacent. It means executing actions whose outcome might develop our wings. Our dissatisfaction with the status quo becomes the cradle for our advancement and helps us initiate our ambitious and bodacious goals.

"If we don't change, we don't grow. If we don't grow, we are not really living. Growth demands a temporary surrender of security."

~Gail Sheehy

I believe that change is the way nature self-corrects the continuity and monotony of life, pushes us out of complacency and into new realms of life, and forces us to unleash new ideas and new discoveries. For instance, a child in the womb cannot remain in the womb indefinitely. No doubt the baby is comfortable in this environment, but nature will, at the right time, initiate change, birthing the child into a new realm, a future that is unknown, yet necessary, for that baby to develop his or her ultimate potential.

I discovered that it's impossible to advance and grow in any area of your life and still step out and try new ways, while maintaining the comfort that existed before the change. Continuing with our baby example, without the child's approval, contractions of the womb will force the baby to descend into the birth canal. Soon, the infant will be forced out of its matrix and into an uncomfortable transition that will not destroy it, but birth it into a new environment. It is change that unlocks the capacity of the child to use its senses—vision, hearing, taste, touch, and smell. All things held constant in the womb, because of the limitation within its environment, the infant will never experience its ultimate potential.

You cannot be so caught up in comfort of what and where you are that you fail to explore the potential of what you can be and where you can go. Do not sacrifice your ultimate greatness at the expense of your present comfort.

The desire to manifest your future must be greater than the comfort of your present matrix.

The wisdom in the Bible talks about ants who store up food during summer in preparation for winter.[1] The ant's ways teach that change is a certainty—you can't avoid it and you can't fight it—so you should prepare for, as well as manage and leverage, change to your advantage. Managing change doesn't mean that you control it, but that you mitigate its implications and steer the process of change to work to your advantage.

"The only secret to change is to focus all of your energy, not in fighting the old but on building the new."

~Socrates

Change might occur spontaneously, such as the unexpected death of a loved one, an acute illness, the sudden loss of a job, or the unplanned blessing of a child. Change might also be self-initiated to create a new outcome for yourself or your organization. Let us say someone doesn't like the way he looks, so he decides to lose a few pounds. He will need to initiate new habits—diet and exercise—that will facilitate his desired outcome. An organization that wants to expand and grow might begin a plan of action, whether it's hiring the right talent or letting go of unproductive employees. While change might occur suddenly, it's best if it is accomplished through a strategic and methodical process.

Most people don't like the process of change, but they enjoy the positive results of change. We want new solutions, but too often we are unwilling to address the old persistent problems that keep us from reaching our potential. But remember, change is inevitable, and successful people understand that change is a necessary disruption for any significant advancement to occur.

You might recall the change from film photography to digital photography. It is a perfect example of innovative change that brought major advancement and shifts in the photography industry. Not only did digital photography change the process, it also diminished much of the cost of producing photographs.

> What happened in the world of photography wasn't just a major improvement. It wasn't just a single evolutionary leap... but Kodak (and Polaroid, among other giants in the field) was hit by revolutionary technological change coming at it from multiple directions: cameras, film, processing, distribution, retailing, marketing, packaging, storage, and ultimately, and most decisively, a radical change in the perception of the market place.[2]

While the change from film photography to digital photography was for some companies a painful disruption, even putting several out of business, the revolution brought about positive change for consumers.

Change Strategy

Strategy is the boat that navigates the seas of the complexity of change.

People oftentimes confuse activity for strategy. Activity is a tactic or action to enhance and deploy the strategy. Strategy is a long-term, logical plan as to how to execute the change. When you change the strategy, you change the results. If you fail to commit to the desired change yet still expect to attain our fullest potential, you deceive yourself. Desired change will not happen by chance. It requires strategy that you are committed to for the long haul. Pursuit and attainment of your ultimate potential requires commitment to significant and calculated change strategy.

Most people tend to blame their environments or circumstances when they don't reach their potential. They even wait for and expect the ideal set of conditions to magically fall into place. Some have a mentality in which they hope one day something amazing will by chance happen that alters their lives. The probability of that happening is like winning the lottery: slim to none. To reach your true potential and develop the capacity to soar to your destinies, just like the eaglet in our previous story, you must determine to make change your ally.

Following are five steps to help you embrace and navigate through change.

1. Develop a Clear Vision
"Visioneering is a clear mental picture of what could be, fueled by the conviction that it should be."

~Andy Stanley

The ability to navigate the challenges of change is made easier by a clear vision—a picture of the life you want to live or the desired outcome for your organization, the values you want to espouse, or even the person you want to become. Most people fail because they have no goals or vague ones at best—they lack a vision. Success requires focus on the big picture, rather than the hurdles you must overcome to reach your goals. Having a clear vision helps to direct the change. It motivates you toward the desired outcome, and it determines the action steps to get there. Vision sets the destination for what the strategy will accomplish.

People don't rally around obstacles and challenges. Rather, a compelling vision motivates them.

Vision becomes your reality. It is said that if you don't know where you want to go, any road will take you there. Before you begin the journey to realizing your ultimate potential and releasing your greatness, you have to determine where "there" is for you. Where do you want to go in life? What is your ideal destination? Who do you want to be? Answering these questions requires deep soul-searching, which will help you clarify what you want your life, or your organization, to look like. Clarity is the sum total of who you want to be and where you want to go. Lacking clarity of your vision risks compromising the resilience you will need to overcome any resistance you may face in your pursuit. Clarity of vision also provides the motivation to make all the necessary sacrifices, because you envision the end results. Clarity eliminates the inability to make decisions.

Change is unsettling only when the destination is unknown. When a captain knows the coordinates of the final destination, he or she can confidently steer the ship accordingly. Even when bombarded by storms, the captain has the drive and equipment to navigate the ship to the desired destination. The ship of change will set sail from the shores of your comfort zone only when you possess a clear-cut vision and are willing to steer toward the vision, no matter what.

2. Own the Change by Leading the Way with Change

"People do not resist change; people resist being changed."

~Richard Beckhard

Change must start with you. You cannot demand of your environment more than you have invested in yourself. You initiate change and give yourself over to being more, going farther, and reaching higher than you ever thought possible.

Organizations, as well as individuals, have to own change and lead the way with change, or else others will outpace them and make them obsolete. Microsoft's acquisition of Nokia is a good example. When Nokia CEO announced the purchase, he said that though the company didn't do anything wrong, somehow they lost.[3] Kouzes and Posner purports in their classic book *The Leadership Challenge* that "Leaders have to prospect the future. They have to be on the lookout for emerging developments in technology, demographics, economics, politics, arts, and all aspects of life inside and outside the organization. They have to anticipate what might be coming just over the hill or around the corner."[4]

The best way to combat change is to lead the way with change.

You must lead the way with change. Do not allow technological advances, new developments, or changing trends force you to change. Pioneers don't simply benchmark other people, companies, or organizations; they set the new standards. Leaders don't wait for change to happen; they lead the way with change. They run toward change. Leaders must be ahead of the crowds, so others will follow them. That means you are either leading change or following a leader of change.

People love to blame circumstances or their environment for why they are not reaching their ultimate potential. To blame competitors, investors, parents, employer, education, genetic disposition, government, the ebb and flow of life, or even technological advances as reasons for your inadequacy is simply self-deception. Challenges are always a part of life. You cannot settle for mediocrity while waiting for all undesirable conditions to somehow dissipate. The change you desire lies within you and begins with you. Own up to the change you desire and lead the way by adapting to new strategies to get where you want to be.

Change in and by itself is not bad. For the most part, your negative perception of change victimizes change and makes it appear to be a negative thing and also influences how you respond or react to it.

Most people are convinced that change is a bad thing, but we need to develop a mindset that managing change will eventually lead to a good outcome. Behavior follows belief, and long-held belief becomes conviction. Welcome the conviction that change is an invitation to potential greatness. Only then will you begin to pursue and initiate change for your betterment. When you become more, you explore your ultimate potential by creating a new reality.

The world benefits from your transformation. This transformation requires sacrifice, dedication in creating the change you want. True change, whether it's individual or organizational, should have at its core not only a desire and drive to benefit humanity, expand global reach, and increase influence, but also personal growth. In other words, motivation for change should be that the transformation will impact humanity and bring about life's advancement.

3. Be Creative and Think Big

The physical world is still there, of course, but our relationship to it is changing fundamentally... Our relationships are increasingly digital, not analog, and our communication is nearly all-digital. We are rapidly changing the filter through which we deal with the world from a physical, material-based perspective to information- and knowledge-based one.[5]

Individuals and organizations must be creative and think outside the box. In fact, thinking should not be linear, but lateral. In today's digital age, we have ever-increasing ways of creating solutions to problems. We must be eager to tackle problems in new ways and ignore the conventional models. We must avoid blind conformity to the status quo, for it is the killer of creativity and potential greatness. If you protect what was, you will fail to embrace what is.

"Fortune does favor the bold, and you will never know what you are capable of if you never try."

~Sheryl Sandberg

Create a habit of learning new ways of solving problems and adapting to new methodologies of doing business. Most people who are accustomed to routine and methodical operation fail to explore the beauty of problem-solving in ways outside the norm. We force solutions and outcomes to develop from old channels and modes of thinking, but to experience change; we must utilize our creative capacity.

When is the last time you did something new? Have you explored new methods of tackling old problems? To be successful, both companies and individuals have to embrace a new way of dealing with complex issues. While you must remain consistent with your vision, do not be infatuated by methodologies.

It takes no skill to sit around and wait for things to happen. But, it takes a courageous leader to anticipate the need for change and take responsibility to initiate solutions to the problems in her life or her organization. For instance, someone brought up in a certain set of circumstances that hindered him from reaching his potential has a choice: blame his circumstances for the outcome of his life and wait for those circumstances to be mysteriously resolved, or look for innovative ways to make a difference in his circumstances and, in the process, do more and be more. People who seek creative ways to birth the change they desire end up tapping into their ultimate potential.

Problems are invitations to innovative big thinking. Seeing problems as problems, escalates the complexities of the situations.

Be open to embracing new ways of solving problems—"outside the box" solutions.

You would do well to find other people who have achieved the outcome you desire and find out how they did it. Creativity will always unleash in the fertile soil of collaboration.

4. Commit to Change and Pay the Price

The next step demands dissatisfaction with complacency. You can't be great and apathetic at the same time. You cannot wish yourself, or your organization, to greatness. Rather, you must believe that you can make the necessary changes for the outcome you want.

Change requires a persistence regarding the continual struggle with the status quo in order to maintain focus of your vision and avoid gravitating to the old, familiar, and comfortable grounds. Guard ferociously your desire to change and intentionally focus on your goals.

You cannot expect greatness without paying a price. Change has a price tag. Leading change comes with a high price tag. What is the cost? It might be emotional, physical, psychological, or financial stress—or some combination of these.

So far, you've made deposits into your "change account." You chose to embrace change and even be a leader in change. You developed a clear vision, and you are thinking creatively and big. Now, you are committed to change. Your account is healthy. But, some people try to fool themselves and expect to withdraw from a change account into which they never deposited. If you want to unlock your human potential, it doesn't come at the price of mediocrity and complacency. It requires being committed to and vested in the person you intend to be.

"Never underestimate the magnitude of the forces that reinforce complacency and that help maintain the status quo."
~John P. Kotter

It's impossible to hang on to who you were, while attaining the fullness of what you ought to be. In other words, you have to leave something behind to become something greater. Don't let your past disappointments and yesterday's failures rob you of your dream potential today. Change is a sacrifice many people living in the present are not willing to make, because it threatens to extinguish how things have always been, which is why most people, even unconsciously, fight to maintain the status quo. Change stretches us, tests our limits, and creates tension, but it's this tension of change that becomes a launching pad to greatness.

Believe in yourself, and pursue the change you want at all costs. Accept that you will have moments of doubt, that you might feel isolated and then begin second-guessing yourself. Consider the caterpillar wrapped tightly in its cocoon. It experiences a period of loneliness in order to develop into a butterfly. The cocoon is a dark lonely place of isolation where potential turns into greatness.

Change requires persistence and commitment to the desired transformation, regardless of the isolation in the process of change.

About a year ago, the organization I lead was facing a choice. Our current facility was too small and we needed to expand into a much larger building, which would enable us to serve more people.

The process required a building that would cost $250,000. Several people were opposed to the move, believing it wasn't necessary to spend that much on a facility that would require renovations. They preferred the easier option of staying in the small building, rather than paying the price for a much larger one that was more suited to our needs. I felt certain of this needed expansion, so I led the way and we completed the building. As a result, those who did not envision the needed change fought against it and criticized the direction we were going. Eventually, some left. Sometimes, change will demand isolation from the critics who don't understand you or your assignment. To lead change, don't pursue the path of least resistance, but go on the path of maximum efficiency, which leads to your potential greatness.

Not everyone is committed to your change, and they will do all they can to keep you stagnant.

5. Change Readiness

"A wise man adapts himself to circumstances, as water shapes itself to the vessel that contains it."

~Chinese Proverb

Personal transparency and self-evaluation of what needs to change is necessary to attain our ultimate potential. Because change disrupts the status quo, it forces you to give up some old, comfortable ideas and ways of doing things. Leadership expert John Maxwell says that a leader must *give up* to *go up*. You must ask yourself: What practices and traditions am I prepared to let go of, in order to go up and embrace the new?

How do you deal with that loss without allowing it to distract you from your ultimate goal? The long-term implication of effective change takes time. It's a journey, a process, not a quick fix; therefore, we must cultivate a change-readiness strategy.

There are three major areas we must be ready to accept change.

1. READINESS TO ADAPT TO NEW METHODOLOGIES

"It is not the strongest or the most intelligent who will survive but those who can best manage change."

~Charles Darwin

Now that you are navigating your desired change, to get to the next level, you have to embrace new methodologies. In a fast-paced world where everything is changing rapidly, one challenge both individuals and organization face is "But we've always done it this way" or "But this is how it has always been." General Stanley McChrystal states the following in his book *Team of Teams*:

> The models of organizational success that dominated the twentieth century have their roots in the industrial revolution but the world has changed. The pursuit

of "efficiency"—getting the most with least investment of energy, time or money—was once a laudable goal, but being effective in today's world is less a question of optimizing for a known (and relatively stable) set of variables than responsiveness to a constantly shifting environment. Adaptability, not efficiency, must become our central competency.[6]

Take for example Blockbuster, the video-rental retail giant that got ousted by a small company no one had heard of called Netflix. Netflix's growth and presence forced Blockbuster to file for bankruptcy. Greg Satell, in his Forbes article "Why Blockbuster Failed and Why It Didn't Have To,"[7] claims that Blockbuster failed, because its leadership had built a well-oiled machine. It was a tight network of extreme efficiency, but poorly suited to let in new information. Blockbuster had a niche, and they had worked hard to build brand profitability, but they failed to recognize the changing trends in their industry. Blockbuster failed to alter its business model—and damage its profitability—in order to compete with the startup Netflix.

Some change can be unsettling because you may feel like you are abandoning the very ideals and values that your life, or your organization, is built on. The reality is, while you must be open to change and new ways of doing things, your core values, or the organization's vision, which are guiding principles, should remain unchanged—but everything else is subject to change.

2. READINESS TO COLLABORATE WITH OTHERS

Greg Satell asserts in his article, "In 2000, Reed Hastings, the founder of Netflix, flew to Dallas to propose a partnership to Blockbuster CEO John Antioco and his team. The idea was that Netflix would run Blockbuster's brand online and Antioco's firm would promote Netflix in its stores. Hastings got laughed out of the room."[8] This partnership would have reinvented Blockbuster and kept them in business longer. To survive changing times, companies have to understand the value of strategic alliances and collaborative partnership. Since 2010, we have seen a major increase in mergers and acquisitions, because companies recognize that their industries and consumers' buying habits are changing and to remain relevant, they must embrace the strength of collaboration with other companies for continued market dominance and relevance.

In today's world, there is a strong network of interconnectedness of individuals and organizations; therefore, it is simplistic to think that you can execute change without the help of others. An old African proverb says that if you want to go faster, go alone, but if you want to go far, go together. In leading change, it's important to recruit those closest to you, including your family. And you must collaborate with people who are more knowledgeable in subjects you need to learn. Those with whom you cooperate help determine how far and how high you go—how much of your dream you attain. You need people who are willing to work with you to achieve your goals. It's vital to build a team of people who can see what you cannot see and have gone where you want to go.

These mentors will improve you, protect your focus, and empower your dreams.

Change requires that you enlist partners or allies who will facilitate the change by either recruiting others, building teams around the new direction, realigning the hearts of your adversaries toward you, or just providing moral support. Collaboration with others also holds you accountable, until you realize the change you are pursuing; otherwise, you might easily slip back into old, failed expectations and habits.

3. READINESS TO EMBRACE NEW COMMUNICATION AND TECHNOLOGY PLATFORMS

In my previous book, *From Dreaming to Becoming*,[9] which contains essential principles for pursuing your dreams, I talk about the importance of assessing the relevance of your dream. Embracing technology should become an important part of pursuing your potential. If you want to pursue your ultimate potential, you cannot insist on the old means and technology that no longer work. Too many people try to hold on to something way too long. For example, not too long ago carrying a boom box was exciting and "cool." To insist on carrying the boom box in an iPhone age is simply ridiculous. We live in an advanced technological world where twelve-year-olds create apps and four-year-olds easily operate computers. Nothing is more powerful as an idea whose time has come. The reverse can be said of an idea whose time has passed. We cannot fight technological advances—it's a losing battle—we must simply adapt. You cannot build a productive strategy to achieve your dreams based on antiquated rules, for the rules of the game are constantly changing, and so should your strategy.

Twenty years ago, most people did not have an email account. Today, most people have more than one, and it's hard to imagine life without email for both business and personal use. Social media platforms like Facebook, Twitter, Linkedin, and YouTube did not exist a couple decades ago, but today, Facebook has approximately 1.6 billion active users who use it primarily for communication. Millions of apps are available that anyone can use to make to tasks easier, faster, and more efficient. General McCrystal confirms this in his book *Teams of Teams*:

> People are more connected, more mobile and move faster than ever before, by lowering what economist call the "barriers to entry"—prohibitive costs associated with entering a market—these changes have ushered in a universe of new possibilities for players operating outside of conventional systems: Mark Zuckerberg, without family connections, starting capital or an undergraduate degree, changed the world before hitting his mid twenties. Justin Bieber posted a self-made video online in 2007 and has since sold 15 million albums accruing close to 200 million in personal wealth. Interconnectedness and the ability to transmit information instantly can endow small groups with unprecedented influence.[10]

Technology is a channel, or platform, which will enhance your capacity and unlock your unlimited potential, which if leveraged correctly will exponentially increase your influence.

In closing this chapter, I would like to emphasize, the word of great UCLA coach John Wooden, who said, "Failure is not fatal, but failure to change might be. Failure to change is often just stubbornness that comes from an unwillingness to learn, an inability to realize that you're not perfect. There cannot be progress without change-even though not all change is progress."[11]

PHINEHAS'S AXIOMS

If you desire to reach your ultimate potential, you must disrupt the status quo and break the nest of your comfort.

- Your dissatisfaction with the status quo becomes the cradle for your advancement and helps initiate your ambitious and bodacious goals.

- The desire to manifest your future must be greater than the comfort of your present matrix.

- Most people don't like the process of change, but they desire to enjoy the positive results of change.

- Strategy is the boat that navigates the seas of the complexity of change.

- Pursuit and attainment of your ultimate potential requires commitment to significant and calculated change strategy.

- The best way to combat change is to lead the way with change.

- Change in and by itself is not bad. For the most part, your negative perception of change victimizes change and makes it appear to be a negative thing and influences how you respond or react to it.

- Change is an invitation to potential greatness.

- People don't rally around obstacles and challenges; rather, a compelling vision motivates them.

- Problems are invitations to innovative big thinking. Seeing problems as problems escalates the complexities of the situations.

- Change requires persistence and commitment to the desired transformation, regardless of the isolation in the process of change.
- The cocoon is a dark lonely place of isolation where potential turns into greatness.
- You cannot build a productive strategy to achieve your dreams based on antiquated rules, for the rules of the game are constantly changing. So should your strategy.
- Technology is a channel, or platform, which will enhance your capacity and unlock your unlimited potential, which if leveraged correctly, will exponentially increase your influence.

5

HONOR:
A MASTER KEY

"Life every man holds dear; but the dear man holds honor far more precious dear than life."

~William Shakespeare

Every human gravitates toward honor, because we were made to be valued and respected. At the core of every human existence is supernatural intrinsic value. Everything you are is a result of what you have chosen to honor; everything you are not is proof of something you have chosen to dishonor. Honor is not only vital, but necessary in attracting the kind of relationships, alliances, opportunity, or even open doors that will cause you to move toward greatness and become your best. Every person, regardless of their background, color, race, nationality, sex, or origin, has some inherent good in them. We each are a masterpiece created with a master plan, and we must seek to find the good in one another. It will be impossible to reach your ultimate potential and achieve greatness if you fail to perceive greatness in others or fail to walk in honor toward other people who are different from you.

The Greek word for honor means to treat someone or something as valuable, precious, or weighty. It is a show of great respect or admiration. Honor has to do with elevating the status of a person or a thing.

My daughter was born into a family of color, for both my wife and I are Africans. At the time of this writing, my daughter is six-years-old and she has not yet learned how to perceive people from their color; she sees everyone as a human being. In fact, without our knowledge, she has often arranged play dates and birthday parties with other kids from her class who are different from her. It always amazed me that whenever I take her to preschool, most of her non-black classmates all play with and love on her. They do not discriminate each other. Children at this age have not learned profiling or prejudice; however, whenever I have met with the parents of these same children, some of these parents would not even acknowledge me or respond to my greetings. I assume it has to do with my skin color.

How you respond to others reveals your understanding and recognition of honor.

Honor is predicated on the understanding that God created all things, and their existence is a revelation of the God factor in them. Therefore, whenever we dishonor people, we devalue God's creation and thus dishonor God. We cannot trivialize people. We must simply learn to elevate and celebrate people and look for the value in them. We have to consistently see people for their potential and not always their faults and shortcomings or even our stereotypes of them. If you have to minimize others to appear great, you are already small. I have come to the conclusion that it is better to assume value in others, than to overlook value in them.

Honor is demonstrated when value is perceived, and dishonor is present when wrong assumptions are made.

Regarding honor, perception is everything. Perception influences honor. Our expectation of people determines their behavior to a great degree. Stereotypes are perpetrated because of prevalent assumptions that most people believe, even though they might be wrong. In other words, people believe what they want to believe. For example, if we believe the assumption that all black men are no good and have potential to commit crime, we begin to expect it, and a good number of black men will live down to our expectations. A somewhat recent example is in America when we saw the dangerous rift that occurred in Baltimore. Young urban black people were rioting and vandalizing property in an attempt to get justice for the murder of Freddie Grey, who was killed while in police custody. The disparity that exists between the police force and these disenfranchised inner-city kids occurs because of wrong assumptions. The young black men are taught to hate the police, and the police are taught to target the young black men as criminals. Are all police officers bad? No. Are all young black men thieves or drug dealers? Unequivocally, no! However, because media portrays this picture, it's what we come to accept.

Everyone rises to perform at the expectation of honor you demonstrate toward them.

A Cultural Dilemma

We don't have to travel far to experience dishonor. Dishonor is everywhere in our society. Dishonor has become a pop culture that many people seem to adore. Children publicly dishonor their parents, businesses dishonor their clients, husbands and wives have lost respect for each other, and our presidents are heckled and booed, while they duck from flying shoes and rotten tomatoes. Politicians name call and all civility has been lost. The person with the best jab gets our vote. Self-interest and meaningless moratorium highjack policies that can benefit many people. Social media offers platforms for millions of views of brawl fights. Tabloids are a billion-dollar-a-year business, while reality shows receive high ratings for their portrayal of scandal, messy lives, and drama. Dishonor is everywhere from the churches to schools, from government to homes, from the workplace to the marketplace.

In case you are unsure of what I mean by dishonor, it is treating something or someone as common or ordinary, even replaceable. Yet, people and certain ideas and traditions should be held as invaluable. As individuals, organizations, and nations, we are incapable of reaching our ultimate potential and greatness when we dishonor the precepts, foundations, people, or relationships necessary for our advancement.

You can trace the rampart growth of dishonor to a leaking foundation of respect.

Most of the disrespect and dishonor we see in today's society may very well be rooted in the poor foundations formed in childhood. The ancient scripture says, "Foolishness is bound in the heart of the child but the rod of correction will drive it far from him."[1] You can't build skyscrapers on faulty foundations, and a broken values-system can never sustain a holistic society. As a nation, we are only as effective morally, socially, or politically as the foundation we lay in our younger generation.

The threat to morality is not the perversion we encounter or the rise of a wrong culture; rather, it's a lack of solid foundation in children that teaches them to discern evil from good and wrong from right. We must admit that we have become a sick society. The cure is not to medicate symptoms, but to eradicate the illness.

Dishonor comes in many forms. It has become popular and is rapidly spreading. We have become a culture dominated by narcissism, cynicism, and selfishness. If we are not careful, we will fall into this culture that opposes honor and displays it as a subservient attitude of the weak. This is one of the big lies of our society. The truth is that showing honor to others is a sign of greatness, not weakness. In the words of Publilius Syrus, an ancient writer, "He who has lost honor can lose nothing more."

While this issue is complex and cannot have a one-size-fits-all solution, we must address this complex issue by looking at a few of the most basic contributing factors of dishonor. The list is endless, so I am not naively suggesting that this list will exhaustively address this matter completely, but shed some light.

1. Breakdown of Family Structure

The lack of parental guidance is the breeding ground that fosters dishonor toward order. This failure of parenthood is a major contributor to the breakdown in society. The failure stems from a variety and combination of factors: negligence, lack of education, poverty, absence of fathers in the lives of children, and the immaturity perpetuated by children having babies. The breakdown of family structure is alarming and plays a role in the failure of family values being instilled or transferred to the next generation.

Absentee fathers have played a major role in the degradation of a society of honor, because fathers are necessary to shaping a child's values. The statistics are alarming when 70 percent of prisoners come from a fatherless home. According to other studies, 71 percent of high school dropouts are from fatherless homes. This lack of education contributes greatly to the proliferation of a culture of dishonor.

Education in and of itself doesn't guarantee honor, but with education comes enlightenment and exposure that fosters conversation, which leads to a shift in the perception and value of something or someone. It allows one to value and explore other schools of thoughts and to engage in healthy, constructive discussions. When we can discuss ideas and beliefs with people who are different from us, we learn to appreciate their opinions, perceptions, and contributions. Then, we can walk in honor toward one another and embrace what others have to say.

2. Failure to Transmit Values to the Next Generation

The ongoing indoctrination of our society through subliminal messages, or conscious and unconscious training, by the media and society in general, has produced an anti-honor culture. The African proverb, "It takes village to raise a child" is obsolete; instead, the perception is "Every man for himself; God for us all." Too few of us are willing to instill values into the next generation, because we are too busy building the present illusion of our lives that we sacrifice tomorrow's reality.

Fewer parents are teaching the lost art of honor; rather, we have accepted the numbing of society with "reality shows," video clips of people fighting, of gaining the advantage over others for personal gain. We know more about Hollywood gossip than we know facts regarding history or men and women who have made and are making positive impacts in our communities. The government will opt to build more prisons than institutions of higher learning, because our priorities are clearly misplaced. When we do not educate and train the young to develop the right values, we have simply relegated them to a life of failure.

3. Democracy

Democracy is great, but, like any good thing, it must have limits and moderations; otherwise, it becomes detrimental. In other words, democracy should never be misinterpreted and used to dishonor the rights of others. We are not to use our free will to violate others' free will. Most of our civil dishonor is characterized as a misuse of "freedom of speech." We have the right to free speech, but it does not give us the right to vilify people or shout so loud as to drown out their voices. If people do not share in our political views, it does not mean that they are less valuable and as such, they are to be treated with dishonor.

4. Increased Access to Information

In the early days before the Internet and free access to information, it used to be that the young would honor the elderly for their wisdom and listen to their sage advice. But now, we have become a know-it-all generation. We "Google" everything and think that we don't need to seek information from others. Before the rise of the Internet, it was customary that those who were more experienced in some way, such as parents and grandparents, would instruct the young. The apprentice would learn from the master craftsman. But, in an era of do-it-yourself (DIY) and self-proclaimed experts, we too easily despise the wisdom of our elders and trust information we cull from impersonal and nebulous so-called authority we find on the Internet.

Don't despise wisdom for information, because wisdom is validated by experience and has been tested through character.

5. Politics

"When there is a lack of honor in government, the morals of the whole people are poisoned."

~Herbert Hoover

Politicians color citizens' perception because policymakers' intentions are always to communicate a higher reality than the present reality. They want to influence behavior that leads to getting votes. I believe that part of the problem of dishonor in the United States of America, and many other countries, is a direct result of bad politics. Politicians who lack civility demean one another and run campaigns of character assassination of their opponents. When was the last time we witnessed a politician running for office solely on values or issues? Instead, we are subjected to a campaign built on attacking the candidates.

While it's healthy to have debates and discourse that engage people in tackling weightier matters, I believe that what we see today on the streets is really the poison from the leadership that has trickled down from religious leaders, professors and teachers, and, most of all, Congress.

Most people don't generally dishonor others intentionally, but dishonor may be predominantly a learned behavior, since we have not taught, and we have not been taught, how to honor one another. I believe that when our leaders model integrity and honor, people will naturally follow suit.

Building a Culture of Honor

To release your ultimate human potential and greatness, honor must not be a good idea, but an ideal principle by which you govern your life.

Everything is better with honor:
- Nations and societies are better with honor
- Businesses and marketplaces thrive with honor
- Schools and institutions are exemplary with honor
- Neighborhoods and homes appreciate with honor
- Marriages are more fulfilling with honor

The Golden Rule

A generally accepted principle is taught in most of all major world religions. Jesus taught His disciples, "Do unto others as we would have them do unto you."[2] I believe that this is a major solution in eradicating the issue of dishonor among human beings. The golden rule is arguably the ultimate peace solution to many of the world's problem. The United Nations recognizes April 5th as the Golden Rule Day. The practice of doing well and seeing the good in others, while rewarding them for their contribution to humanity brings people together.

One organization at the forefront of bringing back and teaching the lost art of honor is iChangeNations (ICN). Under the leadership of Ambassador Clyde Rivers, ICN recognizes common, everyday unsung heroes and honors them for their contribution to humanity with the Golden Rule Award. This award is recognized in over 120 nations and has been presented to people from all walks of life. I have had the privilege of attending and speaking at a few of their annual events where people from several countries around the world gather together and are recognized and honored for practicing the golden rule. In the words of Kevin Gerald, "We must learn to Honor up! Honor Down! Honor All Around."

"You can be deprived of your money, your job and your home by someone else, but remember that no one can ever take away your honor."

~Williams Lyon Phelps

"Before honor is humility."[3] Humility always precedes honor. C. S. Lewis explains humility well: "Humility is not thinking of yourself less but thinking less of yourself." Humility begins with putting others ahead of ourselves. This then sets the way for us to honor others.

Whenever we walk in honor toward others, it transfers the status of our lives into others, and honor applauds others. True honor given to others reveals pure motives toward them. We don't honor people because they are honorable; we honor people, because we are honorable. Honorable people walk in honor toward everyone.

Honor is expressed and demonstrated through actions, rather than words. Living our lives by an honor code is a choice. Our decision to walk in honor is unchanged relative to our circumstances or how people respond to us. Living a life of honor toward everyone is practicing honor up, honor down, and honor all around. Honoring others can lead to doors opening for us and opportunities we might otherwise not encounter. Honor is a master key to greatness, but dishonor brings insignificance. Another way of saying this is that dishonor finds us when we dishonor others.

"No person was ever honored for what he received. Honor has been the reward for what he gave."
~Calvin Coolidge

True honor is not tied to the opportunity we seek, but to the value we bring. Every human is valuable and makes a significant contribution on earth. When we overlook their contributions, we dishonor their potential. When we dishonor people's potential, we terminate their promised futures of who they were created to be. This also nullifies any influence and contribution they would have in our lives in moving us toward greatness.

A principle is at work: honor is almost always met with double honor. Honor attracts abundance. It is a seed that yields more than you sow. From one bean seed a plant grows, which yields numerous beans, each containing several seeds. Taking the opportunity to show honor to others releases honor back to us. The level of integrity in our lives is to a great degree determined by how we choose to walk in honor. Honor will open tremendous doors and cause you to access relationships and people that you were otherwise not in a capacity.

P H I N E H A S ' S   A X I O M S

- How you respond to others reveals your understanding and recognition of honor.
- It is better to assume value in others than to overlook value in them.
- Honor is demonstrated when value is perceived, and dishonor is present when wrong assumptions are made.
- Perception influences honor.
- Everyone rises to perform at the expectation of honor you demonstrate toward them.
- As individuals, organizations, and nations, we are incapable of reaching our ultimate potential and greatness when we dishonor the precepts, foundations, people, or relationships necessary for our advancement.
- You can trace the rampant growth of dishonor to a leaking foundation of respect.
- The threat to morality is not the perversion we encounter or the rise of a wrong culture; rather, it's a lack of solid foundation in children that teaches them to discern evil from good and wrong from right.
- Education in and of itself doesn't guarantee honor, but with education comes enlightenment and exposure that fosters conversation, which leads to a shift in the perception and value of something or someone.
- We are not to use our free will to violate others' free will.

- Don't despise wisdom for information, because wisdom is validated by experience and has been tested through character.
- In order to release our ultimate human potential and greatness, honor must not be a good idea, but an ideal principle by which we govern our lives.
- True honor given to others reveals pure motives toward them.
- Honorable people walk in honor toward everyone.
- Honor is expressed and demonstrated through actions, rather than words.
- Honoring others can lead to doors opening for us and opportunities we might otherwise not encounter.
- Honor is a master key to greatness, but dishonor brings insignificance.
- True honor is not tied to the opportunity we seek, but to the value we bring.

6

❖

STRIVE TO CONNECT EFFECTIVELY

"To be able to communicate effectively not only with an audience, but one to one, goes far toward determining our own success in life."

~Norman Vincent Peale

In my previous book, *From Dreaming to Becoming,* [1] I shared my story of coming to America, including how I survived with only $200 in my pocket. I had arrived in the United States at one of the busiest airports, Dulles International Airport. My ticket was one way, so I had no way of returning home. It was my first time in a plane and my first time out of my village. I had no relatives and no friends in the States. I was on my own to figure out how I would adjust to my new home. I was full of hope. I'd heard, read, and saw in American movies the utopian narrative that led me to believe that if I made it to the shores of this great nation, I would live happily ever after. Granted, I didn't expect my new life in this country of great opportunity initially to be easy, but reality can be a harsh teacher. I did not plan for it to be as dire as it was.

Most immigrants to the United States are in search of that better life, because they have a vision of a desirable future. America promises that with determination and opportunity in this great country, something good will eventually happen to everyone who presses on. Unfortunately, I had no one to guide me and help me navigate the social, economic, cultural, and physical challenges I confronted. My dream suddenly turned into a nightmare. I had been homeless for about two months during my first cold winter on the streets of Harrisburg, Virginia. I had no money for school. At one point, because I could not afford to purchase food, I survived on crackers and coffee for two weeks. No one understood my plight. The college threatened to expel me for nonpayment of my tuition. Upon completion of one semester, that's exactly what happened—I was expelled. My situation seemed to worsen by the day.

I decided to use the last of my money, $88, and relocate to Houston. I purchased a Greyhound bus ticket. Once I had arrived in Houston, I still had several months of struggle, but eventually, I was able to secure a job as a customer service representative, since I had passed the necessary training and qualifications. In fact, I had done such a great job that the quality department used my calls to preview and train new employees on quality assurance.

Through this job, I tried to connect with people I didn't know or have any relationship with. My job was to try to correct whatever issue the callers presented. One very irate client who called in had a major opinion about my accent and asserted herself as being superior, making it clear that she despised who or what I represented. I tried my best to let her words fall away, as I explained the process that would address the reason she called customer service. She continued to be perturbed and very rude. My attempts to communicate with her had fallen on deaf ears. During our conversation, she blurted, "Speak English!" Now, one must be naïve to fail to recognize this kind of bigotry. Although I spoke the Queen's English (British English) all my life in elementary school, high school, and college, she had preconceived ideas that limited her capacity to connect with me.

One barrier in connecting is preconceived ideas. Making wrong judgments and assumptions, or even jumping to conclusions, clouds your perception and affects your receptiveness.

I've shared this part of my personal story to illustrate a point: Even though I had a desire to connect with others, the difficulty was not my lack of communication, but my failure to connect effectively. Sometimes, our attempts to engage and communicate effectively might be met with other challenges, such as others' biases, wrong perceptions, stereotyping, different backgrounds, or other barriers of communication; however, we are to continue to do what we can on our part to attempt to successfully connect with others, regardless of their disposition toward us.

The problem many people face is not a lack of communication, but failing to communicate effectively. Peter Drucker, consultant, educator and author known as the "man who invented management," claimed that 60 percent of all management problems result from faulty communication. In his book *Everyone Communicates, Few Connect*, John Maxwell defines connecting as "the ability to identify with people and relate to them in a way that increases your influence with them. Because the ability to communicate and connect with others is a major determining factor in reaching your potential."[2] Communication and connecting effectively is one of the secrets to maximizing your potential and advancing your influence within your organization, community, and friends. Great communicators have influenced and changed belief systems, even motivated people into massive action. Great speeches like Martin Luther King Jr.'s "I Have a Dream" or Abraham Lincoln's "Gettysburg Address" have called people to arms and even shaped history. Truly, every opportunity to advance to greatness will require you to connect and communicate effectively.

Effective communication almost always influences the outcome of many situations: a job interview, a business negotiation, parenting, governing, diplomacy, pitching an investment opportunity, marriage relationships, and employee-employer relationships, just to name a few. Therefore, the ability to connect and communicate effectively is one of the secrets you must know and an irrefutable skill you have to develop in moving from obscurity to significance. Like anything else worth having, developing effective communication takes effort, determination, and consistent practice. In his book *The Art of Talking So That People Will Listen*, Paul Swets asserts, "Nothing is more essential to success in any area of life, than the ability to communicate well. Nothing can compare to the joy of communicating love, of being heard and understood completely, of discovering some profound insight from another's mind or transmitting your own thoughts to a rapt audience."[3]

Developing your communication skills to be able to connect effectively with us is paramount to your success in life and its significant skill to have in becoming the best you. While this is not a book on public speaking or the art of communication, I have discovered that everyone uses a stage to sell something; it could be their services, their expertise or their products. At one time or another, you will need to develop the capacity to communicate effectively whatever the case may be. From negotiating contracts, empowering others, pitching a business opportunity, soliciting funds, or even casting vision, you must possess the skill of clearly and succinctly conveying your message. Therefore, you must learn the art of connecting. Let's explore how to become an effective communicator and connect with others.

Excellent communicators find great satisfaction not only in communicating their message across but inspiring change and motivating action.

Nine Steps to Connecting Effectively

1. Establish Your Why

"If you don't know what you want to achieve in your presentation, your audience never will."

~Harvey Diamond

Most presenters are so concerned with the nuances and techniques and tools of delivering a speech or a presentation that they fail to focus on the *why* of the message, the purpose of the message. Becoming clear on what the objective of your message is helps facilitate the delivery. Why are you saying what you are saying? What response are you soliciting? What's your message's big picture? What's your objective or desired result? What's the desired final outcome that you are looking for? Why should the listener care and how does it apply to them? So what?

Steven Covey expounds this concept of beginning with the end in mind in his book *Seven Habits of Highly Effective People.* "To begin with the end in mind means to start with a clear understanding of your destination. It means you know where you are going so that you better understand where you are now and so that the steps you take are always in the right direction."[4]

The objective of your speech or communication must be clearer than the style of your delivery. Peggy Noonan, in her book *On Speaking Well*, says, "Style enhances substance: it gives substance voice, it makes message memorable, it makes policy clear and understandable. But it is not in itself the message. Every speech has a job, a reason for being."[5]

I'm not saying that delivery is unimportant—it is. But the importance of establishing the *why* is that it affects the delivery and clarifies the direction of the presentation. At the beginning of every speech or presentation, the audience is eager to hear what you have to say. They will pay attention to your message when your *why* is clear and useful. As an effective communicator, you must not stray from the theme of your message, so that your listeners will understand where your speech or presentation is heading, and then they will be able to apply your message to their circumstances.

The book *Mentoring Matters* states that "the exceptional public speakers rarely have anything to say. They have some kind of idea, which is the most important element of any speech."[6] The first step to good public speaking is to develop an important message. Clearly defining and establishing the *why* of your message helps you create invisible boundaries around your idea, as well as refine and narrow the message to the essential subject matter to be communicated. Once you've determined the purpose of your message, clarify and refine it, until you can state it in a single tweet of 140 characters.

In the book *Splash*, Chris Brady claims the following:

> Until you know what you're shooting at, it's extremely difficult to aim well and you'll have a very hard time getting the audience to follow your line of fire. Envision what you want before you speak, including how you want your listeners to be changed, and then do whatever is helpful in adapting your speech to that goal. Do you want the audience members to know something new when you are done? Or do you want them to feel something they'll never forget ... what do you want them to do differently.[7]

2. Find Common Ground
"It's easy to find reasons for division between people. Finding common ground is harder, but a step towards happiness."

~Author Unknown

When I first relocated to the Unites States, I experienced enormous cultural shock. Everything was so different from the world in which I had been raised. I became so caught up in identifying the differences between both worlds that I was adamant to conform my new environment to my old practices to create a false sense of "safety" from the unknown. For example, I ate at restaurants that had familiar food; I connected with people who came from my country, or at least the same continent. I frantically searched for some familiarity. Everything around me was new and foreign from what I had been accustomed to, and I needed to find something I could identify with. Eventually, I discovered that focusing on the differences between the old and the new, and seeking comfort in the familiar, affected my ability to adapt to my new environment and estranged me from people who didn't talk or look like me. It limited my potential for personal growth and the ability to step into greatness.

Often, whether attending a conference, presenting an idea to a corporate board, or pitching an idea to an investor, most people naturally tend to gravitate to people with whom they share some commonality. While there's nothing wrong with this, don't let this commonality hinder or blind you from opportunities to step into the unfamiliar, even uncomfortable, to share your message. Don't allow fear to rob your discernment for moments and opportunities for greatness. Identifying with your audience's needs creates a direct relationship with them.

There is safety in knowing that you share something in common with your audience or that you both desire an equitable outcome.

In their book *Getting to Yes*, Roger Fisher and William Ury write the following:

> Any method of negotiation may be fairly judged by three criteria. It should produce wise agreement if agreement is possible. It should be efficient. And it should improve or at least not damage the relationship between parties. A wise agreement can be defined as one that meets legitimate interests of each side to the extent possible, resolves conflicting interests fairly, is durable and takes community interest into account.[8]

It's the legitimate interests of each side—the consideration of the community interest, or the speaker and the audience, both sides of a negotiation—that facilitate finding a common ground. John Maxwell sums it this way: "This willingness to see things from other's point of view is really the secret of finding common ground, and finding common ground is really the secret to connecting. It's difficult to find common ground with others when the only person you're focused on is yourself."[9] Therefore, in your effort to become an effective communicator and to connect with others, you must start with their interests.

Whenever you have any communications or a presentation, written or oral, begin by building a bridge, not a wall, and establish a common ground with your audience or your clients. This demonstrates that you care about them and that you have something in common, whether it be a value, a problem, or a goal. Having a common ground establishes your authority to speak into the subject matter.

An effective connector analyzes the audience to discover the unifying experiences that make your audience receptive to your message.

Some factors in determining your audience's common ground include demographics: age, education, affiliations, cultural or ethnic background, and socioeconomic characteristics. In observing these factors, your aim is to identify which elements would affect or inhibit their reception to your message and how to leverage this information to position your message to cater to their realities. According to Orrin Woodward in *Mentorship Matters*, "The main difference between a good public speaker and a great public speaker is his or her ability to read an audience and adapt her speech in real time to fit it needs. Speakers should know their audience and prepare their speeches accordingly."[10]

In analyzing an audience, let's look at an example of how an element such as age group would affect effective communication. For instance, consider communicating or engaging with Gen Y, the group affectionately known as Millennials, people born after 1985. In his book, *Gen Y: Engaging and Impacting This Generation*,

Oscar Amisi points out four major critical shifts that need to happen for us to effectively connect with Generation Y. The first one is to embrace more dialogue. Instead of imposing an opinion over them, you should engage with them in meaningful conversation, which must be fostered with a spirit of inner security. You must be secure enough to allow mature conversation with Generation Y and not interpret their challenging ideas or opinions as disloyalty.

Amisi points out another rung on the ladder of communicating with Gen Ys: vulnerability. These young people will open up to you only when you are vulnerable to share your wounds, failures, and weakness. This vulnerability, he says, is the willingness to be transparent, open, truthful, and tolerant in your conversation with them.

The third significant component Amisi asserts is creating a high trust environment in which Gen Ys can be free to be authentic without fear of being judged, misunderstood, or made to feel insignificant.

Once trust has been established, the greatest communication skill to nurture with this generation is listening—listening with intention of understanding.[11]

3. Care for Others

"The ability to connect with others begins with understanding the value of people."

~John Maxwell

Effective communication starts with showing those whom you seek to communicate with that they are more valuable to you than your agenda or your message.

When you desire to wow the audience and impress them with your oratory skills, you miss out on the greatest opportunity to influence and impact their lives with your message.

We live in a narcissistic, egotistical age, and people have developed an uncanny ability to spot a phony from a far. People will stop listening to you when you care only about yourself. Teddy Roosevelt once wisely said, "Nobody cares how much you know until they know how much you care." Jamie Humes, former speech writer for seven presidents, wrote *The Sir Winston Method.* In it she quotes Churchill: "There is in the act of preparing the moment you start caring. Only then are you ready to speak to an audience. Because the audience can be convinced only when they see you care about what you are talking about."[12] It is caring about your audience, no matter how small or large, that enables them to connect with your message.

Authentic communication is built around mutual concern of those whose attention you seek and whose connection you desire.

It's hubris to think that you can learn or need nothing from others and that they need only what you offer. Seek to know, or the very least consider the legitimacy of others' points of view. It's hard to build deep meaningful conversation with others when all you seek is your self-interest and how to advance your opinions and agenda at the expense of others.

John Maxwell reaffirms this thought that connecting is never about me; rather, it's about the person with whom I am communicating. Similarly, when you are trying to connect with people, it's not about you; it's about them. Before you can connect with others, you have to get over yourself. You have to shift your focus from inward to outward; off of yourself and onto others.[13]

4. Focusing on Your Message Moves You Beyond Your Fears
"The best way to conquer stage fright is to know what you are talking about."

~Michael H. Mescon

Most people have an inherent fear of speaking in public or even to a group of people. In fact, some people fear it more than death. Even the best public speakers who have mastered the skill of delivery are also afraid, to a certain extent, to get up before a crowd. However, fear impairs your ability to communicate effectively. While this fear is natural, you can leverage it by focusing and preparing your message. About focusing on your message to overcome fear, Noonan writes, "When you forget yourself and your fear, when you get beyond self-consciousness because your mind is thinking about what you are trying to communicate, you become a better communicator. Have a text that interests you, it will help you get beyond you, help you focus on your thoughts and not your presentation."[14] If you hone your message and develop clarity, you will lessen your fear level. Carnegie also says, "Only the prepared speakers deserve to be confident. How can anyone ever hope to storm the fortress of fear if he goes into battle with defective weapons, or no ammunition at all?"[15]

Dr. Peter Daniels writes the following in *How to Have the Awesome Power of Public Speaking:*

> In preparing that important speech you must know much more about your subject than what you actually say, and details reflecting the thoroughness of your study will bring an obvious confidence to your manner and tone. When you have prepared by research, attention must then be given to refining the subject matter down to the essentials. Because of the

depth of your preparation and your commitment, then you can be sure that you not only know the road ahead, but you can safely travel on it. [16]

Unpreparedness can add fear when you attempt to speak to an audience on a subject you know very little about. Effective communicators are experts in their subject matter, because they have studied and researched their topic, and they have experience with it. Whatever you speak about, you must have firsthand experience, something you have mastered and have spent sufficient time studying it. Your speech or presentation must become a meaningful "specific," not a wandering "generality."

According to Humes in *The Sir Winston Method*, Churchill suggests that "every formal speech must have two or three points main points that all support one main idea. A speech is like a symphony. It can have three movements, but it must have one dominant melody."[17]

Focusing your message gives it that dominant melody; it narrows your message to your call to action: something you want your listeners to know, do, or believe. As a communicator, you must never sidetrack the audience from your main message or central theme with too much detail. In *Getting Through to People*, author Jesse S. Nirenberg writes, "Talking to the point means communicating only those ideas which contribute to the idea-pattern you're trying to convey. As you feed ideas to your listener, they try to fit them together to form a pattern. Any comment that does not contribute to the other person's understanding of the discussion-objective is beside the point."[18]

5. *Keep It Short, Simple, and Sincere*
"To be simple is to be great."

~Ralph Waldo Emerson

The most effective speech does not attempt to cover the subject exhaustively, but to simply cover three to five main points effectively. Organize what you need to say without rambling. Keeping your message short, direct, and simple gives your message power and significance. According to Humes, "Churchill thought that a speech should look like a radio script, not a newspaper article; it should sound the way you talk."[19] In keeping the message simple, Noonan's advice is that "sentences must be short and concise. Your listeners are trying to absorb everything you're saying. If your sentences are too dense with information, they won't be able to follow. She claims that there is often an unadorned quality to sections of great speeches, a directness and simplicity of expression."[20]

One of the tools in effective communication is simply stating your point clearly, concisely, and in a relatable way. Use points or principles to articulate your message and systematically walk your audience through one point or principle after another. Then, near the end, reemphasize and summarize all points to drive home your message.

John Maxwell also says that making complex subjects simple is a necessary skill if you want to connect with people when communicating. Or, to put it the words of Albert Einstein, "If you can't explain it simply, you don't understand it enough." Greater complexity is never the answer in communication if your desire is to connect with others. People are drawn to people who are warm and sincere, but are repelled by those who are crass and conceited.

6. *Don't Take Yourself Too Seriously*
"Everybody laughs the same in every language, because laughter is universal connection."

~Yakov Smirnoff, Comedian

Keep your presentation simple and add humor, for it touches the audience's emotions, inspiring hope and assisting them in a practical way.

Sometimes, presenters are so uptight with their message and delivery that they heighten the listeners' tension. To put them at ease so that you have their full attention and create that vital connection, interject appropriate humor into your delivery.

Humor is vital and engages your audience both intellectually and emotionally. Humor demonstrates your graciousness to make them laugh, because you are not taking yourself too seriously. Inserting jokes or funny stories seamlessly and naturally into the message to enhance the message without becoming the message.

It's hard to recover from a joke that falls flat, so take considerable care in timing and delivering of the punch line. Avoid off-color jokes and jokes that alienate or denigrate people groups.

7. *Personal Presence*

"Who you are speaks so loudly I can't hear what you say to the contrary."

~Ralph Waldo Emerson

Diana Booher, in *Creating Personal Presence*, says that personal presence involves the following:

- Look—your body language, handshake, movement, dress, surroundings
- Talk—the words you choose, the physical qualities of your voice, how you use your voice
- Think and communicate your thoughts—how you organize ideas and information, what you decide to pass on or withhold, how you frame issues
- Act—the attitudes, values, and competence your actions reveal

Booher continues that as you increase your personal presence, you strengthen your credibility and expand your influence. People with presence look confident and comfortable, speak clearly and persuasively, think clearly—even under pressure. They act with intention. People with presence reflect on their emotions, attitudes, and situations—rather than react to—and then adapt. They accept responsibility for themselves and the results they achieve. Presence has much to do with perception. To be perceived taller, stand tall. Walk, talk, and sit tall by adjusting your posture and using larger gestures.[21]

Most people fail to advance to greatness not because they are incapable, but because they are perceived as incapable. They make the wrong impressions on those able to advance and promote them. An employer might hire a less qualified person, because she or he has greater or better personal presence than the more qualified person who lacks personal presence.

Having personal presence or the lack of it will determine whether you get acknowledged or ignored when opportunity knocks.

Personal presence affects your ability to communicate and connect with others, whether as a group or as individuals. It also impacts your personality and likeability. To move toward greatness, you must cultivate and develop your personal presence by always looking your best. This, in turn, will build more self-confidence and motivate you to advance toward your full potential and open more doors of opportunity. Building on personal presence is a sense of satisfaction and accomplishment, which increases your ability to authentically, confidently, and effectively share with an audience your thoughts and emotions.

8. *Intentional Listening*

"The best speakers are the best listeners."

~Terri Brady

The art of listening is a requirement of an effective communicator. For most people, listening well does not come naturally; rather, it develops through training ourselves to truly hear what others are saying. According to Swets, The Sperry Corporation discovered that without training in the art of listening, most people comprehend only about 25 percent of what they hear. And in both business and personal relationships, the consequences of inadequate listening are extraordinarily costly. In personal relationships, simple listening mistakes can lead to communication failures and the tragic breakdown of understanding between people. One listening mistake after another—slowly, gradually, imperceptibly—can build a wall of resistance between people. Swets suggests six steps in increasing your listening skills.[22]

STEP ONE: CHOOSE TO LISTEN

A good listener chooses to listen deeply, to glean from both the spoken and silent message, the intent and desired response of the person speaking. Your choice to listen facilitates overcoming self-centeredness and focuses your attention on the one talking.

STEP TWO: LISTEN ACTIVELY AND AGGRESSIVELY

Active listening fully engages the mind, and you are concentrating on what is being said. In addition, active listening allows you to provide emphatic feedback, which then encourages the person to go deeper. Active listening affirms the person communicating that they are valuable and what they are saying matters.

STEP THREE: LISTEN FOR IDEAS AND FEELINGS

A good listener is not afraid to genuinely listen for ideas and feelings, to ask for clarification to ensure correct interpretation and understanding of the speaker's intent.

STEP FOUR: LISTEN WITH THE HEART'S "EAR"

Move beyond simply hearing sounds to listening with the "ear" of the heart, which requires both empathy and acceptance. Empathy is walking through experiences in the other's shoes, trying to see the world through his or her eyes, with the sole purpose of understanding the other as fully as possible. Second, maintaining an attitude of acceptance toward the person, even when disliking his or her actions, you are psychologically ready to truly hear the person. This kind of listening requires that you nullify your negative thoughts about the person, so you can be receptive to what he or she is saying.

STEP FIVE: LISTEN TO YOURSELF

If you neglect to know your own mind, to explore your innermost feelings, to thoughtfully consider certain issues, to understand your dreams and ambitions, you will likely fail to "hear" these things from anyone else. The capacity to listen to oneself provides personal integration and psychological readiness necessary to be open or receptive to another point of view. When you listen carefully to yourself, you can see how you come across to other people.

STEP SIX: KNOW WHEN TO KEEP SILENT

Silence is sometimes the best choice. Silence says, "I want to take the time to hear you without interrupting you." "I want to know how you feel about yourself, your failures, your accomplishments, your plans." The most common and serious error of one who wants to help a friend is trying to solve the problem for that person. The misguided helper readily gives advice, instructions, logic, and guidance in hopes of relieving the friend's burden. But, it is supportive silence that many times has the power to help and heal.

9. Practice Your Delivery

"Take advantage of every opportunity to practice your communication skills so that when important occasion arises, you will have the gift, the style, the sharpness, the clarity and the emotions to affect other people."

~Jim Rohn

There are no shortcuts to develop confidence and effective communication. The only way is through continual practice. That's the way to develop confidence and to learn how to communicate effectively. To step into greatness, we must simply develop the capacity to connect with those whom we plan to be in business with, or to get married to, or seek to present our service to, or desire an opportunity from. In the words of Carnegie:

> Don't take a back seat at departmental meetings. Speak Up! Teach a Sunday School class. Become a Scout leader. Join any group where you will have the opportunity to participate actively in meetings. You have but to look around you to see that there is scarcely a single business, political, professional, or even neighborhood activity that does not challenge you to step forward and speak up. You will never know the progress you can make unless you speak, and speak, and speak again.[23]

PHINEHAS'S AXIOMS

- One barrier to connecting is preconceived ideas. Making wrong judgments and assumptions, or even jumping to conclusions, clouds your perception and affects your receptiveness.
- Excellent communicators find great satisfaction not only in communicating their message, but inspiring change and motivating action.
- Becoming clear on what the message is helps facilitate the delivery.
- The objective of your speech must be clearer than the style of your delivery.
- There is safety in knowing that you share something in common with your audience, or that you both desire an equitable outcome.
- Identifying with your audience's needs creates a direct relationship with them.
- An effective connector analyzes the audience to discover the unifying experiences that make your audience receptive to your message.
- Effective communication starts with showing those you seek to communicate with that they are more valuable to you, than your agenda or your message.
- Authentic communication is built around mutual concern of those whose attention you seek and whose connection you desire.

- Effective communicators are experts in their subject matter, because they have studied and researched their topic, and they have experience with it.
- Keeping your message short, direct, and simple gives your message power and significance.
- One of the tools in effective communication is simply stating your point clearly, concisely, and in a relatable way.
- Having personal presence, or the lack of it, will determine whether you get acknowledged or ignored when opportunity knocks.
- Most people fail to advance toward greatness not because they are incapable, but because they are perceived as incapable.
- The art of listening is a requirement of an effective communicator.

7

CULTIVATE AUTHENTIC RELATIONSHIPS

"The most useful person in the world today is the man or woman who knows how to get alone with other people. Human relation is the most important science in living."

~Stanley C. Allyn

Humans are wired for relationships. Relationships influence your mental health and provide a deep meaning and fulfillment in life. Healthy relationships are vital if you want to reach your ultimate human potential, because you cannot attain a significant level of success by yourself. You can only win with others. In the words of English poet and cleric John Donne, "No man is an island, entire of itself."

The most significant investment you will ever make is not a financial one, but rather lifelong relationships. A study conducted by psychiatrist George Vaillant on 268 Harvard undergraduate males from the class of 1938 to 1940 concluded that the "warmth of relationships throughout life have the greatest positive impact on 'life satisfaction.'"[1] Relationships can bring us joy or pain. In times of crisis or difficulty, relationships are shelters where we can lean on others for strength. When opportunities come our way, healthy relationships can be a springboard, a catalyst toward success.

Most successful people can trace their advancements to a special relationship or significant mentorship. Author and speaker Charlie "Tremendous" Jones used to say that the difference between who you are today and who you will be in five years is the people you spend time with and the books you read. Every human being is built to thrive in healthy, authentic relationships.

"People are lonely because they build walls instead of bridges."

~Joseph Fort Newton

The truth is, we are increasingly less prepared to have healthy meaningful relationships, whether it's with our employers/employees, parents or spouses; in our communities, churches, schools; or in politics or business. Most children are taught safety and survival rules. Some are taught to be cautious when encountering people of certain ethnicities. Others are warned to be anti-police, while some are trained to be skeptical of great opportunities. Our eyes and ears are trained to look out for dangerous people and situations, but we are rarely trained to recognize and identify healthy relationships. Placing value in people and relationships is an important factor in having a full and meaningful life.

Most Millennials, and many Gen Xers, garner hundreds of "friends" and followers through social media, like Facebook, Twitter, Instagram, and YouTube; but, generally, they are unable to build authentic, lasting, and effective relationships in the real world. We cannot build genuine relationships from behind a computer. True friendship is not determined by how many "likes" we receive in response to a post on Facebook or how many followers reply to our tweets, which is commonly known as social proof. We have reduced the significance of our relationships to people's momentarily responses to mere posts on social media.

Your influence and significance are not measured by the number of likes and shares on social media.

The truth is, we long for relationship, because we were created to coexist in relationships. Human beings are created to be social. Have you ever considered the fact that the worst punishment handed down to prisoners is solitary confinement? However, in many societies around the world, people willfully practice individualism. They believe they can not only exist, but be successful while living in a private, autonomous, self-made "world" separate from all other human beings. This inevitably gives rise to narcissism. With more focus on self-centeredness and individual accomplishment, a total disregard for others too easily slips in, and the end justifies the means is the operative idea. All of this renders making relationships impossible.

The world we live in today is also one of shrinking personal networks, which explains why many people live in self-imposed isolation, especially when their relationships have been unhealthy and nonreciprocal, leaving them impoverished and hurt. We all desire to have relationships, but building authentic relationship requires us to invest our time and ourselves. Most people are afraid of the work necessary to build true authentic and healthy relationships.

You cannot have a healthy relationship by chance; it is always a result of a committed choice.

How to Build Authentic Relationships

The most successful people understand that they cannot succeed alone, so they have learned the art of forging strategic alliances and significant, authentic relationships. The book of Proverbs says, "He who walks with the wise shall be wise; associate with fools and get in trouble."[2] Use these four steps to develop authentic relationships in your life.

1. Building Authentic Relationships Starts with You

"You can make more friends in two months by becoming interested in other people than you can in two years by trying to get people interested in you."

~Dale Carnegie

A true, authentic relationship is categorized by selflessness. A person who lives for himself will never experience the fullness and value of every relationship. You play the most significant role in every one of your relationships, because the responsibility of cultivating a healthy relationship is not up to others. It has to start with you. The prevailing thought in most people's minds is, "What's in it for me?" But when investing in a relationship, it is imperative that you prioritize the interests of others over your personal interests, preferences, or agenda. The great Zig Ziglar had this philosophy: "You can get anything you want in life if you help enough other people get what they want."

You can cultivate a great, authentic relationship only when you start with self-mastery. Socrates said, "To know thyself is the beginning of wisdom." I believe that to know thyself is the beginning of cultivating a healthy relationship. When we enter into relationships before we know ourselves, we expect the other person to possess what we are deficient in. Then, when we realize they are incapable of meeting our need, both of us become frustrated with the other, and the relationship usually fizzles or blows apart. Remember this: at the onset of most relationships, we don't attract the people who possess character traits we want; rather, we attract people who are just like us. Unless you know yourself, you will demand your associates and friends to satisfy a lack in you that they are incapable of meeting.

Building healthy, authentic relationships with those who will transform your limitations into efficiencies, takes more than attraction; it requires reciprocal investment.

You have to intentionally pursue, cultivate, and invest in such relationships. To only minimally invest in any relationship, but demand the most from others is delusional. You cannot demand a withdrawal from a relationship you have never invested in. Reciprocity is required in every relationship or you will end up bankrupt.

You can't enter into relationships with a *me-first* mentality. You have to be selfless. Most people with a *me-first* mentality are takers who are looking to suck everything they can from every relationship. You can never enjoy a successful relationship with people who secretly wish you to fail in your endeavors, thus making it seem that they are doing better than you are. Whether in business, marriage, career, or any area of life, fulfilling relationships must be mutually beneficial for all parties; it is a win-win situation.

2. Building Authentic Relationships Requires Transparency

"No man can live happily who regards himself alone, who turns everything to his own advantage. You must live for others if you wish to live for yourself."

~Seneca

As you seek to find and build these significant relationships, you must be clear that your motive is not to use others to advance your agenda on their platforms, but to learn and facilitate a synergistic relationship.

Building authentic relationships dictates that all parties should establish their intentions and motives at the onset of every relationship.

One member of the relationship is not as smart as the sum total of all members. Authentic relationships are meant to accomplish something so much bigger than personal agendas and ambitions. So, be transparent as you enter into and remain in these relationships and not try to wear a fake personality in an attempt to fool others into believing something about you that is not genuine.

I am always amazed when I meet protégés around the world who try so hard to impress their mentors or even compete with them. Sometimes, they are trying to conceal their flaws or act as though they have no blind spots, all in an attempt to measure up to their mentors' standards. This doesn't impress me, because anything can be packaged in a nice gift wrap. I am more interested in the content than in the cover. Hiding your flaws doesn't make the flaws disappear. Acknowledging your deficiencies allows you to receive and benefit from the input and wisdom of others. Authentic relationships are meant to grow and develop you.

Every great person depends upon a significant, mutually beneficial relationship. Those whom you rally around will determine how high and how far and how much of your dream you attain. Don't pick just anyone to have a relationship with simply because they picked you; instead, find someone who will bring out the best in you, encourage you to be and do better, and push you toward your destiny. Find people who are experts in your field of interest, people whose presence challenges you to engage your creative capacity. "As iron sharpens iron, so one man sharpens and influences another through discussion."[3] Enter into new relationships in which all parties share common goals. Significant success will come when you link with people of same mindset. You need people in your life who are willing to work with you to achieve your goals, people who are secure enough in themselves to see your dreams realized. You need people in your life you can learn from, who are already successful and won't compete with you.

3. *Building Authentic Relationships Requires Loyalty*
"False friends are like a shade, keeping close to us while we walk in the sunshine, but leaving us the instant we cross into the shade."

~Christian Bover

We give our allegiance or loyalty to what we value. We are loyal to certain political ideals. Some people are loyal to specific cars, others to specific products. Some are intensely loyal to particular sports teams—even if their teams lose game after game, year after year. Regarding relationships, it's impossible for two people to have an authentic relationship without true, ongoing loyalty. In his book *The People Factor*, Van Moody says, "Loyalty is an incredibly powerful force for good in any relationship. In contrast, betrayal is one of the most hurtful and most negative things that can happen between two people."[4]

A relationship cannot be considered *invaluable* when one member of it deems the other person as *replaceable*.

This attitude dooms the relationship, whereas longevity of a relationship is an indication of loyalty. I am perplexed by how loosely people hold relationships and how easily they are prepared to walk away from valuable relationships over disagreements. When you find a great relationship, do all you can to maintain it. In today's world, too many people have become so disloyal and unreliable that it's hard to build authentic relationships.

It's not the true enemies you should fear, but false friends who masquerade as loyal confidants with a goal to make you fail to reach your ultimate potential. To fully benefit from every strategic relationship, fierce loyalty is the main ingredient. There is a difference between people who are *with* you and people who are *for* you. People who are *with* you stick around as long as it benefits their agenda, but people who are *for* you are loyal to you, even when they have nothing to gain from their loyalty to you.

4. ***Building Authentic Relationships Requires Losing Your Luggage***
I often travel by air. Recently, I flew to Columbus, Ohio. I had two bags, a smaller carry-on, and my metal display banner. Unfortunately, I could not keep it with me, so I had to check it along with my two bags. The first bag cost me $25 to check, the second $35, and the third one, the banner, $125! Regardless of how light the item was, the airline charged this fee, because it was a third checked item. I grumbled to myself about this, but the more I thought about it, the more I realized that paying a higher price for excess baggage is a principle in real life: the more baggage of past hurts and disappointments we carry with us, the higher the price we have to pay in terms of bad attitudes, fears, and unfulfilled goals. Author Glenn Clark advises, "If you wish to travel far and fast, travel light. Take off all your envies, jealousness, unforgiveness, selfishness, and tears."

If you desire to have healthy relationships, your desire to be loved must be greater than your fear of being hurt.

In order to build healthy relationships, you must overcome certain fears and the pain of past hurts. If you refuse to deal with lingering pain from your past, you will fail to maximize your full potential and greatness, or enjoy the full benefit of your relationships. You cannot remain incarcerated by painful past experiences and at the same time be free to enjoy reaching your fullest potential. Did you catch the contradictive words in that sentence? *Incarcerated* and *free*. If you live in one state, it is impossible to live in the other. You are either incarcerated or you are free. Which one do you want to live in? You must learn to forgive and let go of the past, so you can enjoy the present. Unforgiveness will stunt your growth and limit your ability to reach your full potential. Welsh poet, orator, and Anglican priest George Herbert once said, "He who cannot forgive others breaks the bridge over which he must pass himself." You have either a great past and a small future or a small past and a great future. But, you have to choose to embrace that where you have been is not greater than where you are going. It's not so much your relationships that hold you back from your destiny; rather, it's the significant relationships you know you need that you fail to explore for fear of a wrong outcome.

PHINEHAS'S AXIOMS

- Your influence and significance are not measured by the number of likes and shares on social media.
- You cannot have a healthy relationship by chance; it is always a result of a committed choice.
- A true, authentic relationship is categorized by selflessness. A person who lives for himself will never experience the fullness and value of every relationship.
- You can cultivate a great, authentic relationship only when you start with self-mastery.
- Building healthy, authentic relationships with those who will transform your limitations into efficiencies takes more than attraction; it requires reciprocal investment.
- To only minimally invest in any relationship, but demand the most from others is delusional.
- Building authentic relationships dictates that all parties should establish their intentions and motives at the onset of every relationship.
- Those whom you rally around will determine how high and how far and how much of your dream you attain.
- You need people in your life who are willing to work with you to achieve your goals, people who are secure enough in themselves to see your dreams realized.
- A relationship cannot be considered invaluable when one member of it deems the other person as replaceable.

- It's not the true enemies you should fear, but false friends who masquerade as loyal confidants with a goal to make you fail to reach your ultimate potential.
- If you desire healthy relationships, your desire to be loved must be greater than your fear of being hurt.
- You cannot remain incarcerated by painful past experiences and at the same time be free to enjoy reaching your fullest potential.
- You have either a great past and a small future or a small past and a great future.
- It's not so much your relationships that hold you back from your destiny; rather, it's the significant relationships you know you need that you fail to explore for fear of a wrong outcome.

8

FOLLOWERSHIFT

"Trapped within every follower is an undiscovered leader."

~Dr. Myles Munroe

One of the most important secrets to stepping into your greatness is learning the skill to follow others who have been successful, or those who are willing to mentor and coach you into greatness. There is an old saying that says, "If you see a turtle on a fence post, you know he had some help." You must simply learn the art of following if you intend to be at the fencepost of greatness or accomplishing something significant. How you follow today will influence how you lead others tomorrow, because great leaders model for their followers what true leadership looks like. Whether you are a coach, teacher, scout leader, community leader, or business manager, the impact of leadership is reflected by the quality of one's followers. The ultimate goal of followership is for a follower to develop into an effective leader.

A quick search on Google on the topic of "leadership" produces more than 750 million hits. Leadership is a diverse and complex subject on which numerous books have been written. In this chapter, I would like to divert away from the mainline teaching that presupposes leaders are superior to followers and that everyone ought to be a leader with an understanding of the nuances of leadership. I would like to take you through a paradigm shift on followership—a mental shift on becoming an effective follower—hence the title of this chapter. A great leader is always first a great follower. In fact, your leadership pattern traces back to your path as a follower.

Effective followership can develop and enhance one's capacity to lead. Every follower has an instinct for leadership, an inherent desire or longing to lead in some way. However, everyone is not privileged to have had a great foundation on which to develop their leadership capacity. Some people lack true leadership models—whether it's a great father or mother, a coach or mentor, or a teacher—to invest in them, to develop their leadership capacity. This means they are encumbered to develop themselves as leaders.

Most books on leadership assume readers understand and possess the fundamentals of leadership and need not explore followership, but to reach your potential and unlock your full capacity as a leader, you must first develop your ability to follow effectively. The ability to lead can be traced back to Genesis 1:26, where God said, "Now we will make humans, and they will be like us. We will let them rule the fish, the birds, and all other living creatures" (CEV). This biblical story reveals God's original plan was for humans to rule, govern, control, and even manage His Creation.

God gave us the capacity and responsibility to lead, protect, and cultivate everything He had created. Our ability to lead is then tied to our ability to follow the sovereign leader, God, and to learn the pattern of leadership from the Creator's laws and principles that govern the environment over which He placed people. As the story unfolds, we learn that our original ancestors' inability to follow effectively led to their demise and the loss of their position of authority and rulership. When the original intent for humans to rule and govern was destroyed, they lost their identity, and, as a result, instead of ruling, they became subordinate, and humanity entered the struggle to dominate one another. This led to some people being leaders and others followers.

What Is Followership?

It's important to define *followership*, because this concept has been maligned and misunderstood by many people. Today's social media influence is measured by "likes" and "following." It is presumed that the more followers you have, the more influence you have. Following in this context is reduced to and limited to a moment of social engagement or interaction when one chooses to follow another on a social media platform. While social clout may appear to reflect one's influence, it's truly not a measure of the value of his or her impact as leader. In other words, this is not what we are talking about regarding followership.

People tend to follow other people and ideas they find fascinating, and they follow causes and organizations they believe in. Who you follow identifies whom, or what, you have chosen to be influenced by.

Jimmy Collins, founder of Creative Followership and former Chick-Fil-A COO, defines a follower as someone who has chosen a leader.[1] In her book *Followership: How Followers Are Creating Change and Changing Leaders*, Barbara Kellerman defines a follower as the response of those in subordinate position (followers) to those in superior ones (leaders).[2] For the purpose of this chapter, let's combine both definitions and refer to *followership* as a follower's response to a leader's influence.

When you submit to other leaders and follow them well, you position yourself to become an effective leader. In *Attitude and Altitudes*, author Pat Mesiti states, "An effective leader is not someone who is loved or admired, but someone whose followers do the right things."[3] Effective followers are proof of effective leadership.

Some people believe that being a follower is being less than, that a follower cannot be a leader. I assure you that nothing is farther from the truth, because everyone is a leader in one area and a follower in another; a mentor in one area, but a protégé in another. We need to overcome the disposition that being a follower is a "less than" position. In the words of Jimmy Collins, "A stronger leader requires a stronger and smarter follower to successfully support and execute the necessary tasks. It requires no less intelligence, strength, fortitude, or maturity to follow than it does to lead."[4]

"Civilization is always in danger while those who have never learned to obey are given the right to command."

~Bishop Fulton J. Sheen

In the fourteenth and fifteenth centuries, the concept and practice of apprenticeship emerged. In apprenticeship, an experienced craftsman would take on a young male or female and provide room and board, basic education, and training in a specific craft. The apprentice began training somewhere between the ages of ten and fifteen, and would continue for at least seven years. Apprentices lived in the masters' homes until they honed their skills and became a journeyman and later, a master craftsman.

In our modern time, Olympic athletes borrow from the apprenticeship model. These athletes often leave their families, or even their countries, to train with a coach for countless hours, even years, to become Olympic medalists. In the same way, a follower who is willing to sit under and learn from leaders—mentored—he or she will develop and become equipped for greatness.

Greatness is not accidental; it's a choice, a conscious decision that one makes to emerge out of mediocrity into significance.

Integration of Followership and Leadership

Because the relationship between followership and leadership is so tightly intertwined, we need to study the role of leaders in developing good followers, who will then become superior leaders.

If ever we needed role models, it's today. Young people need adults who are great role-models, provide direction, and are good examples of great leadership. Upcoming entrepreneurs are looking for mentors to guide them through their many decisions that can mean the difference between success and failure. Most marriages are starving for insight, desperately needing advice to build healthy relationships. True fathers are missing in homes, the political world is in disarray for lack of leadership, and the next generation is ill-prepared to carry the baton. We need people who are intentionally committed to help take others from obscurity to greatness.

The absence of authentic leadership is so alarming that people are willing to follow charlatans.

Numerous books have been written on leadership, being a great leader, and discovering the leader in you, but you'll find very few on effective followership. Everyone wants to be a captain, but no one wants to be the crew. However, it seems no one is preparing others to realize and maximize their potential as effective followers. Perhaps it is because many have made following, or being a follower, as something negative. Some definitions of leadership describe following as a less-than trait. Or maybe we perceive following to have emerged from the hierarchical leadership structure in which the people at the top—leaders—make all the decisions and those who are at the bottom—followers—have no say or influence.

Whether it is a gaggle of geese that rotates leadership, a pack of lions in the wild hunting, or a business or organization, the reality is that everyone can't lead at the same time. In his book *Tribes*, Seth Godin says, "The merits of leadership are so ingrained that its, natural to say, 'I'll take the lead.' Sometimes, though, it may make more sense to take the follow. Leading when you don't know where to go, when you don't have the commitment or the passion, or worst of all, when you can't overcome your fear—that worse of leading is worse than none at all. It takes guts to acknowledge that perhaps at this time, right now, you can't lead. So, get out of the way and take the follow."[5]

Every leader starts out as a follower at some point in their lives. To be a leader you must first follow, learning from others who precede you. If you are incapable of being a great follower, you will never be a great leader. One of the most effective ways to train others is to follow the facilitators and observe what they do. This is called *shadowing*. We can apply this same concept to following. You know you are a successful leader when your followers start leading others.

"The signs of outstanding leadership appear primarily among the followers."

~ Max Dupree

True leadership is revealed by one's ability to serve others and to train and develop his or her followers into becoming servant leaders. Great leaders not only lead, but also serve. Nelson Mandela, Martin Luther King Jr., and Mother Teresa are just a few great leaders who served their generation. They were willing to stoop low and raise others to greatness. We must shift away from developing tyrant leaders and bosses and toward cultivating compassionate servant leaders who are not jealous or intimidated or insecure, but reach down to others and raise them up to success. One is simply not remembered for the title or position she had, but for the impact she made.

Followers tend to live up to the expectations of leadership modeled for them. Strong leaders develop strong followers, but weak leaders suppress the followers to make them dependent upon them. It's my belief that anytime you see weak and suppressed followers, it's a result of a lack of true leadership. You can tell a great leader from his attitude while serving others. Great leaders are interested in adding value to their followers. Bill Hybels describes leadership as leading people from here to there; it's leading people from where they are to where they ought to go—even when they don't want to.

Your greatest investment as a leader is in your followers, training them to replace you when you exit your leadership position. True leadership is about unlocking the latent potential in your followers and to empower them to become great leaders. In the words of Sheri L. Dew, president and CEO of Deseret Book Company, "True leaders understand that leadership is not about them, but about those they serve, it's not about exalting themselves, but about lifting others."[6]

If we don't teach people that it's okay to follow and learn from others, we will automatically limit their potential for greatness. No one can succeed in life alone. I recall watching a documentary about geese flying in formation. As each goose flaps its wings, it creates uplift for the birds following. By flying in a V formation, the whole gaggle adds an additional 71 percent flying range, than if each bird flew alone. Whenever a goose falls out of formation, it suddenly feels the drag and resistance of trying to fly alone and quickly returns to the formation, taking advantage of the lifting power of the birds immediately in front. This principle in nature is true in leadership: when you follow leaders who have preceded you, you add to your success potential and obtain the lifting power to go farther and reach higher, than you would on your own.

10 Qualities of an Effective Follower

Let's turn our attention back to being a follower. Though not listed in order of significance, these are several qualities to embrace in becoming an effective follower and stepping into greatness.

1. *Self-Awareness*

An effective follower must be secure in himself. It is paramount that followers know who they are apart from their roles in their organizations, their careers, their possessions, and their leaders. Warren Bennis commended that to "Know thyself, then means separating who you are and who you want to be from what the world thinks you are and wants you to be."[7] Self-awareness is a conscious state of self-discovery regarding one's strengths, capabilities, gifts, weaknesses, personality, character, passion, and experience. Self-awareness brings knowledge to the fact that while you seek to unleash your potential; you are limited in some areas and cannot be great at everything. One difference between an effective follower who develops into an effective leader and a mediocre follower is a better perspective and a healthy self-awareness.

You were created to lead in an area of gifting. If you find your gift, you will find your area of leadership potential.

Many people fail to realize, and thus maximize, their potential because they compare themselves with others and worry too much what other people think of them. When you don't value yourself and all you have to offer, you become anxious to impress and live up to the expectations of others.

Sometimes, people overlook their best qualities and try to work on fixing their weaknesses. The challenge with working to develop your weaknesses is that you can never develop them to the extent of exceeding your strengths. Self-awareness helps you to master your strengths and gifts, while not majoring on your weaknesses. This makes you a confident person rather than insecure, which reduces the need to compete against your fellow followers or even your leaders.

To lead others, you must first lead yourself. It's impossible to manage others, while mismanaging yourself. Thomas J. Watson, former chairman of IBM once said that, "Nothing so conclusively proves a man's ability to lead others, as what he does day to day to lead himself."[8]

"You must have the courage to be true to yourself."

~Coach John Wooden

When you are true to yourself, you will be true to others. An effective follower's courage will arise from an internalized discovery of self, which creates a strong, positive self-confidence and security in one's purpose. Your true value is not in your title or position or current function; rather, it comes from your self-awareness that you are inherently a leader, even when you are following someone else.

True leaders can function without a position. Leadership is not about position but about disposition.

The need to minimize or unfavorably compare yourself with those whom you follow comes from a lack of understanding personal self-worth. The insecurity of feeling second class or not knowing who you truly are will lead to failure as a follower and ultimately, as a leader. These insecure leaders feel the need to control, to call all the shots, and to oversee everything.

When you begin with yourself, being aware of your inadequacies as well as your strengths, you naturally affect others and allow others to positively affect you. Beginning with self-awareness helps you to overcome fear and gain genuine confidence simply because you have full knowledge, conviction, and confidence in your natural abilities. It also helps you conquer jealousy, because you are sure of your value, which can only be developed through knowing that you are shaped for significance. It also ignites a sense of fulfillment. You do not need to compete with others, because you understand your uniqueness and authenticity.

2. *Shared Vision*

The basis of an effective relationship between a leader and a follower is a shared vision. A sensible, clear, and concise direction that is measurable, consistent, and achievable. It is difficult to enlist and recruit followership without it. A shared vision unifies the leader's goals and the follower's ambitions. In the words of Howard Schultz, executive chairman of Starbucks, "When you're surrounded by people who share a passionate commitment around a common purpose, anything is possible."[9] In the Bible, we're told that "two cannot walk together unless they agree" (Amos 3:3).

Leaders must know, communicate, and clarify the direction the business or organization is heading to enable others to follow. Every leader is responsible to provide clarity to the vision in a manner that elicits corporate and individual followership, because it is difficult for followers to maintain commitment when they are not clear on the vision. In addition, the leader must clearly convey what the win looks like.

Followers must believe in and trust in the leader and his or her vision, even though they might differ on the methods of accomplishing it. They are wise to study the leader's vision and understand where their vision and the leader's vision intersect. Followers are more motivated to work together with a leader when they know that their contributions are adding value to their overall personal vision, as well as the corporate vision. Kouzes and Posner, in their book *Leadership Challenge*, admonish, "No matter how grand the dream of an individual visionary, if others don't see in it the possibility of realizing their hopes and desires, they won't follow voluntary or wholeheartedly. Leaders must show others how they, too, will be served by the long-term vision of the future, how their specific needs can be satisfied."[10]

"The growth and development of people is the highest calling of leadership."

~Harvey S. Firestone

Followers want to work for a leader who is building or growing something that fosters measurable success toward the followers' desired goals too, which encourages followers to know that they are not only making progress, but also making a difference through the shared vision and growing and developing their capacity to become effective leaders. An effective leader desires to support the dreams, aspirations, and goals of their followers.

3. *Sustained Commitment*

One of the greatest leaders ever to live is arguably Jesus of Nazareth. Jesus led a group of twelve men, whom He invited to follow Him on a journey of transformation that would later impact these followers and ultimately make a significant difference in the world. These twelve men, eleven of whom later became known as apostles, were instrumental in the propagation of the Gospel to most of the known world.

On one occasion, He invited someone to follow Him. This man answered, "Yes, Lord, *I will follow you, but first let me say good-bye* to my family." But Jesus told him, "Anyone who puts a hand to the plow and then looks back is not fit for the kingdom of God."[11] Clearly, this man wanted to be a follower, but he wanted to tie up any loose ends and possibly sought his family's approval before he proceeded further. A true follower understands the value of reckless abandon—being willing to let go and overcome present challenges or inconveniences because of an anticipation of getting to a desired future.

A true follower doesn't follow when it's convenient; rather, he or she possesses a conviction, with a sustained commitment, to follow a group, a cause, or a person, despite all odds and challenges he might face.

True following is not conditional, based upon favorable circumstances, but out of conviction.

In the words of Ken Blanchard, "There is a difference between interest and commitment. When you're interested in doing something, you do it only when it's convenient. When you're committed to something; you accept no excuses—only results."[11] Sustained commitment means staying true long after the excitement has faded, holding on in spite of everything. It's the ability to push through difficulty, knowing that victory is imminent. Therein lies the distinction between true followers and fair-weather followers, because very few people are committed to staying with a leader or cause long enough to extract the value of that relationship.

"Success seems to be largely a matter of hanging on after others have let go."

~Williams Feather

Commitment is costly. Commitment requires faithful adherence to the decision one has made, in spite of obstacles that occur. Many people fail to realize their potential, because when it comes to the demands of commitment, they are not willing to pay the price to be everything they are purposed to be. Effective followership demands sacrifice and commitment. Greatness will demand of you more than your initial expectations. It means a disruption, it means an inconvenience to your daily routine, and it means going an extra mile. It's impossible to experience your full potential with half-hearted commitment. However, these sacrifices will eventually unlock the follower's potential and cultivate what it takes to be great.

As an effective follower, your sustained commitment to a leader, a group, or a cause is critical to the development of your leadership capacity. Every follower is capable of cultivating, growing, advancing, and expanding their leadership capacity, but this requires a continual commitment to the work of developing personal capacity. Most people fail to develop their true potential, because they are unwilling to remain committed to a leader, group, or cause long enough to explore their true potential. To be all you were meant to be and to explore the value of every leader-follower relationship requires sustained concentration and focus on the goal, which is the development of your capacity. As it's worth repeating that followers don't follow when it's convenient; rather, they follow from conviction, with an unwavering commitment, despite all odds and challenges they might encounter.

Effective followers desire to submit, learn, and grow through their commitment to a process and to a person. Commitment comes from knowing why you are following. The objective of following a leader must be established at the beginning of every relationship. You follow others with an intention of developing your capacity, not a motive to advance your personal agenda. When from a self-promoting agenda people join a leader and they discover that they are unable to realize their agenda, their commitment to that leader is compromised.

You follow others with an intention of developing your capacity, not a motive to advance your personal agenda.

4. *Student of Learning*

"Great coaching is helping people discover what they already know."

~ Bill Gove

It's impossible to unlock your full capacity without a teachable attitude or a learning mindset. A hunger for learning leads to personal growth and development. Your leadership potential develops organically out of your natural tendency to learn and apply what you learn. It is not enough to just be taught leadership; it is a concept that should be caught. Any true follower must listen, learn, and apply the advice offered by a proven leadership. Learning must be a way of life that a true follower embraces, in order to reach the upper echelons of influence and leadership. There is always something to learn from those who have preceded you in your leadership journey. Personal growth is a lifetime endeavor.

You must always be learning, acquiring knowledge, and seeking wisdom, regardless of how much you know.

A teachable spirit is a willing attitude to learn what you might already know, but from another person's perspective.

Great leaders tend to be some of the most coachable and open-minded people you will ever meet. If all you know is all there is to know, then that's all you will ever know. A follower who is willing to learn is a thousand times better than a leader who thinks he or she knows it all. In his book *Leadership Gold*, John Maxwell says that the greatest obstacle to discovery isn't ignorance or lack of intelligence; it's the illusion of knowledge.[13]

"The only fool bigger than the person who knows it all is the person who argues with him."

~Stanislaw Jerzy Lec

Too often, preoccupation with self limits personal growth; however, a true follower will embrace a leader as one assigned to facilitate, guide, and provide the necessary influence for change needed in discovering his or her potential. To unlock your full potential and scale great heights of success, you must abandon the belief of superiority, which makes you see others as inferior, and not only listen to the advice and wisdom of your leaders, but also follow it. Great followers practice the philosophy of *once a student always a student*, understanding that education and insight can come from any source. When you are teachable, you are able to learn from the viewpoints of others, to explore issues from different perspectives. In addition, you come to appreciate other people's knowledge, vision, and creativity. In the great words of Coach John Wooden, "It's what you learn after you know it all that counts."

Andy Stanley, in his book *Next Generation Leader*, says, "You will never maximize your potential in any area without coaching. It is impossible. You may be good. You may even be better than everyone else. But without outside input, you will never be as good as you can be. We will do better when someone else is watching and evaluating."[14] Effective followers reproduce the values of their leaders, because they are willing to embrace these values through coaching/mentoring.

5. *Shadow the Leader*

Effective followers are not a replacement of their leader's legacy; rather, they are an extension of their leader's influence.

Ralph Waldo Emerson once said that an "institution is the lengthened shadow of one man." This means that institutions, as well as individuals, magnify the leader's character, principles, values, and reputation. One of the most important decisions a follower can make is to select the right leader to shadow. It is paramount that effective followers are willing to observe, study, learn from, and know their leaders very well. The leader's influence must be replicated and displayed in the followers' actions. This doesn't mean a follower becomes a carbon copy of the leader. It means that a leader's influence should be revealed when the follower properly shadows the leader. Shadowing the leader is not a follower's lack of autonomy, but proof that the follower is a true student of the leader. In *Creative Followership*, Jimmy Collins writes, "Becoming a part of the right shadow gives followers instant credibility they otherwise might not possess."[15] Great followers never compete with their leaders; rather, they complement them. They study their leaders to observe what they do and how they do it—not just the methodology, which is imperative, but also the principles that govern why they do what they do.

Mimicking leaders without understanding their hearts or the premise behind their decisions does not yield lasting impact. Collins continues to say that followers must know their leaders, learning all they can about their leaders' strengths, talents, likes, and dislikes.[16]

Another facet of great followers is figuring out their leader's weaknesses and how they can help the leader succeed. An effective follower discovers what the leader does not do well, and then takes on the obligation to do what their leader does not like to do.

6. Sincere Humility
"Pride leads to destruction; humility leads to honor."

~Proverbs 18:21 (CEV)

Humility is a word, even a trait that is almost extinct in this generation. Few people want to take the humble position of a follower or servant leader. Some associate humility with weakness. Humility is not being a doormat so people can walk all over you and abuse you to their advantage. Neither is humility an underestimation or an overestimation of yourself. "True humility," said Rick Warren, "is not thinking less of yourself; it's thinking of yourself less."[17] When you think of yourself less, you open yourself to learning from others, for it allows room for growth, and it allows you to consider others' perspectives.

In his book *The 7 Habits of Highly Effective People*, Steven Covey says, "The person who is truly effective has the humility and reverence to recognize his own perceptual limitations and to appreciate the rich resources available through interaction with the hearts and minds of other people. That person values the differences, because those differences add to his knowledge, to his understanding of reality. When we're left to our own experiences, we constantly suffer from a shortage of data."[18]

Great minds emerge from the accumulation of collective thoughts and insight of others.

If you want to gain insight from others, you must be sincerely humble and willing to learn. Arrogance may make you feel superior, but it makes you despise the wisdom of others, including their knowledge and insight. Arrogance clothes you with a "I know it all" mindset that will never help you develop as a leader. Humility is demonstrated not only in how you treat people, but also in how you perceive them. True greatness and humility assumes that everyone you meet has invaluable insight. Humility in a follower is a sign of maturity. Humility is the ability to harness appropriately your knowledge, and it is the power to learn from others.

A great leader cannot advance if surrounded by passive followers.

7. Self-Initiative

A fundamental character and indicator of competence of an effective follower is one who takes initiative. One of the challenges for most followers, which also can limit their ability to realize and maximize their potential, is the expectation that it's someone else's responsibility to voluntarily teach them the principles and offer them the wisdom necessary to succeed. Sometimes, followers even mistakenly believe that an act of God should change their circumstances without any effort or minimal investment on their part. Most followers are waiting for mentors to approach them about being their protégés, but it doesn't work that way. Many followers want to benefit from areas and relationships in which they have not made any investments.

Being an effective follower means that you must be proactive: get up and do what needs to be done. Effective followers take the initiative to pursue great leaders; they don't wait to be pursued. They cannot wait for information and resources to get to them. If they want or need something, they know it's up to them to take the appropriate action, even if it's something they have never done before. An effective follower is willing to invest time, finances, and resources in their own development. Self-initiative is proof to a leader of your desire and passion, for it reveals your commitment to the process.

"Success depends in a very large measure upon individual initiative and exertion, and cannot be achieved except by a dint of hard work."

~Anna Pavlova

Live with expectation that it's your responsibility to pursue every opportunity and relationship. Mary Kay Ash, founder of

Mary Kay Cosmetics, is quoted as saying, "There are three types of people in this world: those who make things happen, those who watch things happen, and those who wonder what happened." Effective followers take self-initiative and make things happen—and not just for their own benefit.

Every effective follower must invest in every significant relationship before he or she can make any withdrawals.

In the words of Zig Ziglar, "We can have everything we want in life if we help other people get what they want." Effective followers never look at a relationship with a leader with the attitude of "What's in it for me?" Instead, they take initiative to help their leaders get to their goals first, to solve their problems first, then the leader is able to reciprocate by helping followers accomplish their goals and dreams.

Effective leaders start with their followers' interests in mind, and effective followers start with their leaders' interests at heart.

Effective followers work to change and improve their leader's organization, circumstances, and even personal lives for the better.

They assess problems before they arise, anticipate challenges, and seek to alleviate and solve the problems for their leaders, while also responding to opportunities. In the same way, effective leaders help their followers expand their capacity and reach their potential. They cultivate trust by allowing their followers to take initiative without feeling threatened by their followers' attempts to advance themselves or their organization. Truly great leaders encourage and build their followers to initiate. Great leaders and organizations create a framework that does not limit self-initiative, but encourages followers' creativity.

8. *Strength*

Followers must develop mental toughness and emotional resilience. They cannot be fragile, seeking to quit every time the going gets tough. They cannot afford to get caught up in the emotions when leaders offer feedback and instructions. The object of followership is the personal development of their leadership capacity; hence, they might encounter more correction and character building than accolades.

Followers who desire acknowledgment more than they desire development are not ready to be effective leaders.

Effective followers have the fortitude to take tough criticism and strong correction, yet keep on ticking. They focus on logical solutions and then move on to the next challenge.

No leader wants followers who function only when acknowledged or celebrated. John Wooden, Hall of Fame basketball coach, said, "You can't let praise or criticism get to you. It's a weakness to get caught up in either one."

9. Stayers

The continued effectiveness of leaders is greatly influenced and determined by the loyalty, faithfulness, and staying ability of the followers who surround and support them. Effective followers are committed for the long haul. Active followers are sold out to the shared vision, but they are also truly committed to their leaders.

There is a difference between people who are with you and people who are for you. Most times people stay with a leader as long as it benefits them and their agenda, but authentic followers are for the leader, even when they have nothing to gain from their loyalty. What good is it to follow a leader halfway, and then abandon the very mission you gave yourself to accomplish? A great follower stays with the leader long enough to see their vision become their reality.

10. Servanthood

Effective followership is a result of a servant's heart and desire to be humble enough to consider the needs of your leaders and others around you above your own interests or desires. Effective followers don't serve with intention to draw attention to themselves, but seek to see the accomplishment of the shared vision and assignment of their leader or the greater goal that they seek to establish. Whether you are a follower or a leader, you are never too big to serve others. I heard of this saying by Rory Vaden, "That if serving is beneath you then leadership is beyond you." A great follower treats everyone as a valuable leader in the making. At any given time, we are subordinates to someone else and it doesn't make you less than.

PHINEHAS'S AXIOMS

- A great leader is always first a great follower. In fact, your leadership pattern traces back to your path as a follower.
- Effective followers are proof of effective leadership.
- Who you follow identifies whom, or what, you have chosen to be influenced by.
- Everyone is a leader in one area and a follower in another; a mentor in one area, but a protégé in another.
- Greatness is not accidental; it's a choice, a conscious decision that one makes to emerge out of mediocrity into significance.
- The absence of authentic leadership is so alarming that people are willing to follow charlatans.
- If you are incapable of being a great follower, you will never be a great leader.
- How you follow today will influence how you lead tomorrow, because great leaders model for their followers what true leadership looks like.
- Strong leaders develop strong followers, but weak leaders suppress the followers to make them dependent upon them.
- True leadership is about unlocking the latent potential in your followers and to empower them to become great leaders.
- You were created to lead in your area of gifting. If you find your gift, you will find your area of leadership potential.
- Self-awareness helps you to master your strengths and gifts, while not majoring on your weaknesses.
- It's impossible to manage others, while mismanaging yourself.

- True leaders can function without a position. Leadership is not about position, but about disposition.
- True leadership is about unlocking the latent potential in your followers and to empower them to become great leaders.
- If we don't teach people that it's okay to follow and learn from others, we will automatically limit their potential for greatness.
- A shared vision unifies the leader's goals and the follower's ambitions.
- It is difficult for followers to maintain commitment when they are not clear on the vision.
- You follow others with an intention of developing your capacity, not a motive to advance your personal agenda.
- It's impossible to experience your full potential with halfhearted commitment.
- Your leadership potential develops organically out of your natural tendency to learn and apply what you learn.
- A teachable spirit is a willing attitude to learn what you might already know, but from another person's perspective.
- True following is not conditional, based upon favorable circumstances, but out of conviction.
- Effective followers are not a replacement of their leader's legacy; rather, they are an extension of their leader's influence.
- Shadowing the leader is not a follower's lack of autonomy, but proof that the follower is a true student of the leader.
- A great leader cannot advance if surrounded by passive followers.

- Great followers never compete with their leaders; rather, they complement them.
- Great minds emerge from accumulation of collective thoughts and insight of others.
- True greatness and humility assumes that everyone you meet has invaluable insight.
- Effective followers take the initiative to pursue great leaders; they don't wait to be pursued.
- Self-initiative is proof to a leader of your desire and passion, for it reveals your commitment to the process.
- Every effective follower must invest in every significant relationship before he or she can make any withdrawals.
- Effective leaders start with their followers' interests in mind, and effective followers start with their leaders' interests at heart.
- Great leaders and organizations create a framework that does not limit self-initiative, but encourages followers' creativity by setting limits or boundaries on far they should go.
- Followers who desire acknowledgment more than they desire development are not ready to be effective leaders.
- Great followers stay with the leader long enough to see the vision become their reality.

9

———— ✦ ————

PRACTICE SIMPLE DISCIPLINES

I have never been to a chiropractor, but a recent conversation with a chiropractor-friend gave me a new perspective. He said that the body will often get out of alignment, causing certain bones in the body structure to become dislocated or skewed. The body will accommodate these changes and will still function, yet at a nominal level. This situation calls for a chiropractor to adjust these bones to realign them. You don't want just anybody doing this, for it takes an expert or someone who understands the ideal body structure to realign the bones, so the body can go back to function in its optimal level.

Our conversation continued, and I learned that once the body is in proper alignment, certain simple disciplines and exercises can maintain the proper adjustment and avoid the body's defaulting to wrong posture or a less than optimal performance. Not only does one need to follow through by doing the exercises, but also regular visits to the chiropractor is recommended to keep the bones aligned, thus avoiding the dysfunction and accompanying discomfort or pain.

Just like it takes a chiropractor to realign the body's bones to their ultimate potential, a few simple disciplines will keep you on the path to optimal performance and maintain your course, as you journey from obscurity to greatness. If you fail to maintain these disciplines and are unwilling to do what is necessary to succeed, you will find yourself operating below your potential and experiencing minimal results. In *Good Great*, Jim Collins asserts, "Much of the answers to the questions of 'good to great' lies in the discipline to do whatever it takes to become the best within carefully selected arenas and then to seek continual improvement from there. It's really just that simple. And it's really just that difficult."[1]

Bob Proctor, in his book *The Art of Living*, observes, "The truth is, discipline is the ability to give yourself a command and then follow it. You will never develop anything of consequence if you are not disciplined. If you are disciplined, you can have most anything you want. This is so basic, it's so simple and yet it's so misunderstood. Most people go through their entire life and never enjoy what they could enjoy because they lack discipline… If you want to make any significant change in your life, you absolutely must command yourself to do what you know has to be done and then follow through."[2]

"What great accomplishments we would have in the world if everybody had done what they intended to do."

~Frank Clark

Certain simple disciplines are necessary for stepping into greatness, but they are also the easiest *not* to do. But when you practice them consistently, you are sure to have the most impact in advancing toward greatness. Big changes sometimes follow small disciplines. The following disciplines are necessary to stay in the "true north" path, as you move from obscurity to greatness. Remember, these are not optional behaviors recommended for you to choose from; rather, they are consistent imperative disciplines that must become a part of your daily life. These disciplines are to be observed, especially when you feel like you don't "feel" like it.

1. Simple Discipline of Compounding Effort

"In all human affairs there are efforts, and there are results, and the strength of the efforts is the measure of results."

~James Allen

Nothing will happen to a dream you do nothing about. Most people know their desired destination, but are not willing to walk the walk that leads them toward greatness. Instead, they only talk about it.

Though the promise of desired outcomes is fascinating, too often people fear the process it requires to get there. To succeed in anything, you must continuously put in the effort before you can expect any results. The path to greatness is a toll road that demands payment—in this case, time and energy. The farther you desire to go, the more tolls you must pay to advance toward the destination.

"If you add a little to a little and then do it again, soon that little shall be much."

~Hesiod

There must be corresponding actions that move you closer toward greatness. Having the desire alone and hoping and wishing alone cannot advance you out of obscurity and into greatness. It's a common saying that nothing ventured is nothing gained. Where you have nothing to lose by taking steps that could lead to success, then by all means, put forth the effort to get there. Winston Churchill said, "Continuous effort—not strength or intelligence—is the key to unlocking our potential." Greatness requires ongoing advancement from a life of mediocrity and obscurity to a life of significance. If you stay with the process long enough, your desired outcome will always be inevitable. Results will always rise proportionately to match your continuous effort. Long-time accomplishments are a result of compounding short-term efforts.

Greatness doesn't happen in a day; it a result of daily cumulative and compounding efforts.

Zig Ziglar tells a story that is applicable to our subject and best illustrates this concept of compounding effort:

> Several years ago two friends of mine, Bernard Haygood and Jimmy Glenn, were driving in the South Alabama foothills on a hot August day. They were thirsty, so Bernard pulled behind an old abandoned farmhouse with a water pump in the yard. He hopped out of the car, ran over to the pump, grabbed the handle and started pumping. After a moment or two of pumping, Bernard pointed to an old bucket and suggested to Jimmy that he get the bucket and dip some water out of a nearby stream in order to "prime" the pump. As all pumpers know, you must put a little water *in* the top of the pump to "prime" the pump and get the flow of water started. In the game of life, before you can get anything *out* you must put something *in*...When you put something "in," the law of compensation says you'll get something "out."

> Well, let's get back to my friends in South Alabama. South Alabama is hot in August and after a few minutes of pumping, Bernard worked up a considerable sweat. At that point he started asking himself just how much work he was willing to do for that water. He was concerned about the amount of reward he would receive for the amount of effort ex-

pended. After a time he said, "Jimmy, I don't believe there's any water in this well." Jimmy replied, "Yes, there is, Bernard; in South Alabama the wells are deep and that's good, because the deep well produces the good, clean, sweet, pure, best-tasting water of all." Jimmy is also talking about life, isn't he? The things we have to work for are the things we appreciate most.

By now Bernard was getting hot and tired, so he threw up his hands and said, "Jimmy, there just isn't any water in this well." Jimmy quickly grabbed the pump handle and kept pumping as he said, "Don't stop now, Bernard; if you do, the water will go all the way back down and then you'll have to start all over again." That, too, is the story of life. There isn't a human being in existence, regardless of age, sex, or occupation, who doesn't occasionally feel he might as well "stop pumping" because there isn't any water down there. So if you occasionally feel that way, it should be comforting to know that you've got *lots* of company.

There's no way you can look at the outside of a pump and determine whether it will take two more strokes or two hundred more to bring forth the water. There's often no way you can look into the game of life and determine whether or not you'll get the big break tomorrow or whether it will take another week, month, year or even longer.

Regardless of what you are doing, if you will pump long enough, hard enough and enthusiastically enough, sooner or later the effort will bring forth the reward... Fortunately, once the water starts to flow, all you have to do is keep some steady pressure on the pump and you'll get more water than you can use. This is the story of success and happiness in life.[3]

2. Simple Discipline of Decision-Making

"It's not what's happening to you now or what happened in your past that determines who you become. Rather, it's your decisions about what to focus on, what things mean to you, and what you're going to do about them that will determine your ultimate destiny."

~Anthony Robbins

Great people understand that the decisions they make today will shape their future. Your life results don't come from seemingly unrelated decisions or events. Every decision is moving you toward greatness and closer to your destiny, or further from whom you were intended to be. Jeff Olson observes the following in his book *The Slight Edge*:

The right choices and wrong choices you make at the moment will have little or no noticeable impact on how your day goes for you. Nor tomorrow, nor the next day. No applause, no cheers, no screams, no life-or-death results played out in Technicolor. But it is precisely those very same, undramatic, seemingly insignificant actions that, when compounded over time, will dramatically affect how your life turns.[4]

Your ability to move toward greatness and maximize your potential requires a developed ability to make great decisions.

Great people have learned the art of decision-making. They can make decisions quickly, but change their minds slowly. These great decisions are not solely a result of assessing facts, gathering information, understanding issues, accumulation of evidence and knowledge, or the elimination of wrong options; rather, they are the product of developing a continual capacity and mental fortitude to make right decisions. This comes from having learned to establish a philosophy that is developed from experience of making both right and wrong decisions. William Clement Stone underscores this truth in his book *The Success System That Never Fails*:

These personal experiences will indicate that each new decision that a child or an adult makes in a given set of circumstances begins patterns of thought that later create a tremendous impact in his life. When an adult makes a decision, it's likely to be foolish or sound, depending on his past experience in coming to decisions.[5]

If you never attempt to make decisions for fear of making the wrong one, you cannot develop good decision-making skills. Acquire these skills by starting with simple decisions: What will I eat today? What will I wear? The daily practice of making decisions trains you to make bigger and better qualitative decisions that lead to greatness.

"The road to the performance of great things must always lead through the performance of partial tasks."

~Ludwig von Moses

In *Attitudes and Altitudes*, Pat Mesiti says that procrastination will not lead you to your destiny or build the lives of people around you. I have often said that the greatest ability a human being has is the ability to decide. But, the greatest inability is indecision. Both have powerful consequences. There can never be opportunity unless a decision is made. Mesiti's approach to decision-making is to ask yourself the following questions:

1. *Am I the right person to make this decision?* Am I too emotionally involved, or emotionally uninvolved?

2. *Is the objective of the decision clear?* Is what I want to achieve clear enough in my own mind to make a decision?

3. *Am I acting or reacting?* Am I acting on the basis of the betterment of others? On the betterment of my organization, or the future success of my life? Or, am I reacting in anger and raw emotion?

4. *Have I considered all options?* Have I asked the "for" and "against" questions? Do I have the game plan to follow through on my decision? A good decision-maker requires a sense of judgment, and judgment is a simple choice between different options.[6]

Decision-making is not an easy straightforward process. You might have to use various methods of sound decision making to bridge the gap between where you are and where you want to go. One approach to decision-making is SWOT: Strengths, Weaknesses, Opportunities, and Threats. This analysis helps you determine the best possible outcome. Another technique is FILOP, a method for ethical decision-making, which reviews the Facts, Issues, Law, Options, and Principles of the issue. Some decisions must be evaluated considering the future: Will this decision yield similar results, while upheld over time?

Another decision-making process is to reevaluate your past decisions in similar matters. Determine any trends or patterns, as well as the impact of the results, whether positive or negative. Study other people's processes who've made similar decisions. What did they base their decisions on? What were the results?

Sometimes, you will be forced to make a decision by merely focusing on the facts, regardless of how you feel emotionally.

Finally, the urgency of some decisions demands that you go with your intuition or instincts. Some decisions, even important ones, must be made in a split second, like a quarterback who has only seconds to decide the play with all the changing variables, as the players break the huddle. The value in any decision made is in its implementation and some decisions have to be made spontaneously.

3. Simple Discipline of Practicing Effective Habits

"Successful people are simply those with successful habits."

~Brian Tracy

Author Dr. Robert A. Russell said that developing greatness in one's life is simple; anyone can do it. You merely do little things in a great way every day. Good or bad, habits have enormous power to shape the outcome of our lives. Whenever we repeatedly do something, or behave a certain way, it soon becomes a habit. A habit is an action that has become automated.

Lewis Howes, in his book *School of Greatness*, says this:

> Here is the thing about positive habits: It isn't that important which habits you practice, as long as they are beneficial, and they work for you. What matters is that you commit to them and that you do them every day. Practicing positive habits is about committing to a routine. A routine guaranteed to move you closer to greatness.[7]

Champions have champion habits. The old saying "Champions don't become champions in the ring; they are merely recognized there." If you fail to put in the work of training yourself through the power of habit, you will fail to develop the capacity to emerge into greatness. You don't achieve greatness in a day. It is developed through daily habits. It is said that the secret of one's future can be hidden in their daily routine. You cannot keep doing what you have always done and yet demand different results. Begin today to establish non-destructive habits that lead away from mediocrity and toward greatness.

Greatness is not birthed out of good intentions, but through consistent positive habits.

Zig Ziglar writes in *Better than Good*:

> Habits are one of the critical components in the life of every person alive today. The problem is that habits can be good or bad, constructive or destructive, positive or negative, encouraging or discouraging. If we are going to live a "better than good" life, you must build as many positive habits into your life as possible. Think of your life as one of those giant cables on the George Washington Bridge and every individual wire is a habit. The more positive habits you bundle together, the stronger your life becomes—the more traffic it can bear, the more storms it can withstand and the more service it can provide to others. I have never known a true peak performer who did not invest consistent energy into the cultivation of good habits.[8]

Following are some effective habits to consider developing, as you activate your potential and move toward greatness.

- The habit of listening
- The habit of learning
- The habit of reading
- The habit of time management
- The habit of doing your best
- The habit of health
- The habit of rest

- The habit of self-discipline
- The habit of going the extra mile
- The habit of pure thoughts
- The habit of generosity

The Habit Poem

I am your constant companion.

I am your greatest helper or your heaviest burden.

I will push you onward or drag you down to failure.

I am completely at your command.

Half the things you do, you might just as well turn over to me,

and I will be able to do them quickly and correctly.

I am easily managed; you must merely be firm with me.

Show me exactly how you want something done, and after a few lessons

I will do it automatically.

I am the servant of all great men.

And, alas, of all failures as well.

Those who are great, I have made great.

Those who are failures, I have made failures.

I am not a machine, though I work with all the precision of a machine.

Plus, the intelligence of a man.

You may run me for profit, or run me for ruin; it makes no difference to me.

Take me, train me, be firm with me and I will put the world at your feet.

Be easy with me, and I will destroy you.

Who am I?

I am a HABIT!

~Anonymous

4. Simple Discipline of Excellence

"The quality of a man's life is in direct proportions to his commitment to excellence."

~Vince Lombardi

At the beginning of this book, we learned that greatness is not a destination; it's a continuous state of being, a progressive achievement toward excellence and away from a life of complacency or mediocrity. The acceptance of a lower level of excellence is mediocrity, and mediocrity stifles greatness.

Pat Riley, who is known as one of America's best coaches, wrote the following in his book *The Winner Within*:

> Complacency is the last hurdle any winner, any team must overcome before attaining potential greatness. Complacency is the success disease: it takes root when you're feeling good about who you are and what you've achieved. The temptation to slack off starts when you're feeling good about who you are and what you've achieved. After you have spent yourself emotionally and physically to achieve the great dream, it's so easy to accept the illusion that your struggle has ended. The congratulations of your friends and family—and maybe even the media—all help you believe that you will stay high on the pinnacle right where you belong. You've arrived. And it feels so great to let go of yesterday's hunger and insecurity. From that enticing moment forward it gets harder and harder to make sacrifices ...while you are celebrating success, someone else is laying plans to move up in the world and you better know it.[9]

Sometimes, people who don't have the same conviction as you will attempt to stifle your growth, or even your desire, from obscurity to greatness. You must remember that excellence will never ever compromise to accommodate its critics. Your pursuit for excellence will not be valued by everyone, especially those who lack similar conviction.

When people don't understand the level of your convictions, don't expect them to value your commitment to excellence.

Are you accepting less of yourself than you are capable of being and doing? As you progress in the journey toward greatness and away from obscurity, you must possess a relentless desire to go further than you ever have, to be more and reach higher than you ever thought possible. Excellence is simply a belief that whatever you engage in, you can always make it better. A commitment to excellence is not a result of chance, but a choice that everyone seeking to step into greatness must make.

It's impossible to attain greatness without a commitment to excellence.

Denis Whitley shares a story about a craftsman who autographed his work in excellence:

> In 1644, a child was born. He lived to be 93 at a time in history when the average life span was but 35 to 40. He taught himself his trade and began his career.

He often worked alone with primitive tools, but his focus every day was to put the best he had into his work. The man-made violins. He labored over each and every process and step to ensure that he had "autographed" them with excellence and the best that was in him. He created his own personal standard of excellence for his craft, and he actually signed his name on each instrument that passed the test. Today, some three hundred years later, the name of this craftsman who was committed to excellence is the benchmark for the best in musical instruments. His name? Antonio Stradivari! His Stradivarius violins sell for hundreds of thousands of dollars because they are the best. When Stradivari labored, he did not know of the legacy he was creating. He was doing his best, day in and day out, to reach his standard of excellence. He didn't spend the extra time and care to get the accolades of upper management or to be the top producer in the company. He did it because excellence was part of his focus, mission, and obsession.[10]

In today's market, one of the most expensive Stradivarius violins was sold for $16 million. The way to be invaluable and memorable is to create a legacy of excellence in every undertaking. My philosophy is this: if anything is worth doing, then it's worth doing right or not worth doing it at all.

"Do the best you can until you know better, then when you know better, do better!"

~Maya Angelou

5. Simple Disciplines of Patience and Perseverance

"By perseverance, the snail reached the ark."

~Charles H. Spurgeon

We live in a microwave generation. We value instant over process. But very few worthwhile things happen instantly, and when they do, they are short-lived and disappear as quickly as they came. Likewise, things without significance in our lives have no staying power.

Greatness is a process that demands patience and perseverance. You will not attain significance overnight, so you must learn to trade impatience for perseverance. It's easy to desire greatness, but hard to travel the path to greatness. No one knows how long this inconvenient path will take. When greatness is not imminent, most people acquiesce to the challenges and bow out of the process, or even consider changing the path. Sometimes, circumstances or events force you to start over… several times. You might even come to a complete halt, or life will throw a punch that threatens to cripple your desire to continue on the path. Numerous detours will challenge your view of greatness and try to extinguish your desire.

But, hold fast to your commitment and keep moving toward your goal.

Chances are that greatness will take longer to achieve than you initially expected. It is possible the journey will be harder than you thought, but never give up. Refuse to quit, and stay the course no matter how hard it gets. It's easy to get disheartened in your pursuit of greatness, but you must resolve never to give in to the discouragement or give up on the process. Too many people give up too soon and they never experience greatness. Develop your mental and emotional fortitude to overcome the hardships that threaten your success, as you press on the path toward greatness.

Few people have suffered through personal and professional loss like Abraham Lincoln did. Through patience and persistence, he preserved through some of the most difficult conditions.

* ❖ 1831: failed in business
* ❖ 1832: defeated for the legislature
* ❖ 1833: failed in business again
* ❖ 1834: elected to legislature
* ❖ 1835: his sweetheart died days before their wedding
* ❖ 1836: he suffered a nervous breakdown and was bedridden for six months
* ❖ 1838: defeated for Speaker of the House
* ❖ 1840: defeated as an elector
* ❖ 1843: defeated for congressional nomination
* ❖ 1846: elected to Congress

- ❖ 1848: defeated for Congress
- ❖ 1855: defeated for Senate
- ❖ 1856: defeated for vice president
- ❖ 1859: defeated again for Senate
- ❖ 1860: elected president of the United States

Most people would have given up after only a couple of failures, but he persisted. Today, he is arguably one of the greatest presidents ever to serve. At what point of Abraham Lincoln's journey would you have given up? The truth is that most of us would have abandoned our ambitions, because of the pressure and the weight of our circumstances. Winston Churchill said it best, "Never give in. Never, never, never, never—in nothing, great or small, large or petty—never give in, except to convictions of honour and good sense. Never yield to force. Never yield to the apparently overwhelming might of the enemy." Churchill had his share of critics, but he didn't listen to the naysayers. Never adjust your dreams to accommodate your circumstances or your critics.

Samuel Chand, in *Leadership Pain*, writes the following:

> To persevere, we need a vision for the future that's bigger than our pain. We may not see it clearly, and we may not like the process of getting there, but we have to be convinced in the depths of our hearts that enduring the pain will someday be worth it. This confidence enables us to raise the threshold of pain so we can respond with courage and hope.[11]

Your desire to manifest what you expect must be greater than the pain of the process, if you want to stay on the path to greatness. The way to greatness has no shortcuts. So persevere, because the process is equally as important as the outcome you desire.

Angela Duckworth's research about those who join the United States Military Academy is amazing. Each year in their junior year of high school, more than 14,000 applicants begin the admission process. This pool is winnowed to just 4,000 who will receive nomination into the academy. Slightly more than half of those nominees, about 2,500, meet West Point's rigorous academic and physical standards. From that select group, just 1,200 are accepted. And yet, one in five cadets will drop out before graduation. What is more remarkable, she says, is that historically, a substantial number of dropouts leave in their first summer, during an intensive seven-week training program named *Beast Barracks*, or simply *Beast*.

According to Duckworth's research, those who were highly accomplished were paragons of perseverance. They were the opposite of complacent. Each was chasing something of unparalleled interest and importance, and it was the chase—as much as the capture—that held the gratification. In sum, no matter the domain, the highly successful cadets possessed a kind of ferocious determination that played out in two ways. First, these exemplars were unusually resilient and hardworking. Second, they knew in a very deep way what they wanted. They not only had determination, they had direction. It was combination of passion and perseverance that made the high achievers special. In a word, they had grit.[12]

"Success seems to be largely a matter of hanging on after others have let go."

~William Feather

6. Simple Discipline of Pursuit of Focus

"An unintentional life accepts everything and does nothing. An intentional life embraces only things that will add to the mission of significance."

~John Maxwell

It's harder to hit a shifting target. Most people fail to achieve greatness, because of broken focus. In other words, they let distractions steal their focus. If you want to accomplish greatness, you must limit your distractions. You must be totally dedicated to removing distractions and maintaining focus, if you desire to step into greatness. Greatness demands concentrated energy and focus. This means giving up on things you love to focus on the main goal you desire to actualize.

Distractions are not always bad things, but sometimes, a good thing at a wrong time can be a distraction. Learn to minimize distractions by being intentional on curbing out of your priorities, activities, people, and things that steal your focus. Designate specific times that you devote in pursing the things that matter to you and that which will bring greatest return on your path to greatness. It's important to rule out what you do poorly, or less effectively, and concentrate your creative energies on what you do best only.

Jim Collins, in his book *Good to Great*, explains the famous essay "The Hedgehog and the Fox" by Isaiah Berlin, who divided the world into hedgehogs and foxes, based upon the ancient Greek parable. "The fox knows many things, but the hedgehog knows one big thing." In this parable, the fox tries to use cunningness to catch the hedgehog. It uses all the tricks it knows. It sneaks, races, and even plays dead, yet every time the hedgehog defeats it, the fox goes away with a nose full of spines. While the fox attempts all these different things, the hedgehog knows how to do one thing well: how to defend itself.

Berlin extrapolated from this little parable the principle of dividing people into two basic groups: foxes and hedgehogs. Foxes pursue many ends at the same time and see the world in all of its complexity. They are "scattered or diffused, moving on many levels," says Berlin, never integrating their thinking into one overall concept of unifying vision. Hedgehogs, on the other hand, simplify a complex world into a single organizing idea, a basic principle or concept that unifies and guides everything. It doesn't matter how complex the world, a hedgehog reduces all the challenges and dilemma into simple—almost indeed simplistic— hedgehog ideas. For a hedgehog, anything that does not somehow relate to its idea holds no relevance.[13]

Collins's conclusion is that "every company [or individual] would like to be the best at something, but few actually understand—with piercing insight and egoless clarity—what they actually have potential to be the best at and, just as important, what they cannot be the best at. And it is this distinction that stands as one of the primary contrast between the good-to-great companies and the comparison companies."[14]

Greatness demands singleness of purpose and laser-like focus.

If this is true of companies, it's true of individuals. Just as the hedgehog is good at one thing, defending itself against the fox, each of us must determine the one thing we will be great at. This one thing distinguishes us from the many things that seek and fight for our attention. Most people are fascinated with many things and even other people. They spread themselves too thin trying to be everything to everyone. They chase whatever infatuates them, instead of marrying their dream. They attempt to pursue several dreams and goals simultaneously, rather than giving themselves fully to one thing.

I would rather have one dream that defines me, than many that are vague and unfulfilled. You must decide where your passion lies and what your true potential is for being great, then stay true to it.

Author Harry A. Overstreet observed, "The immature mind hops from one thing to another; the mature mind seeks to follow through."

7. Simple Disciplines of Speed of Execution

"Create a definite plan for carrying out your desire and begin at once, whether you are ready or not, to put this plan into action."

~Napoleon Hill

The key to advancement toward greatness is by rigorous speed of execution and implementation of strategy through action. Good thoughts without actions are as detrimental as bad thoughts with action. Turn your desire for greatness into an actionable plan. Successful people are willing to translate their desires and goals into reality through execution.

The final, and most important, discipline I recommend is the ability to execute. Execution is different from merely just taking action. Execution assumes a strategy. It's impossible to hit a target you are not focused on. This is not a game of chance or Russian roulette; rather, you have loaded then aimed at your goal. You cannot accomplish every good random idea and still be the greatest at one thing.

Brian Dodd introduces the acronym AIM in his book *10 Indispensable Practices of the 2-Minute Leader*: *Activate,*

Integrate, and Mobilize. "AIM requires activating a plan, integrating resources at hand, and mobilizing people or your team to effectiveness. It's all about coordinated execution—putting a strategy into motion, pulling essentials together and leading a team forward. Taking AIM is not a one time, one track exercise, but an ongoing challenge on multiple platforms. But taking AIM is crucial to hitting targets and achieving goals."[15]

"Without strategy execution is aimless. Without execution strategy is useless."

~Morris Chang

Constantly reevaluate what you are taking AIM at before executing. The strategy on what to execute on will evolve from your disciplined pursuit of focus: zero in on your passion and determine the one big thing you have potential to be great at. It takes countless hours of pursuing your passion before you can step into greatness.

The 4 Disciplines of Execution states that human beings are genetically hardwired to do one thing at a time with excellence.

> Execution starts with focus… One prime suspect behind execution breakdown was clarity of objective: People simply didn't understand the goal they were supposed to execute… The first discipline is to focus your finest effort on one or two goals that

will make the difference, instead of giving mediocre effort to dozens of goals.[16]

According to the authors, the greatest challenge you face in narrowing your goal is saying *no* to a lot of good ideas, even some are great ideas. "Nothing is more counterintuitive for a leader than saying no to a good idea, and nothing is even a bigger destroyer of focus than always saying yes."[17] You will always have more good ideas than you have capacity to execute. Once you've established your strategy, execution is the only logical next step. Remember, great people are remembered not because of the dreams they had, but for the ones they accomplished.

"A strategy, even a great one, doesn't implement itself."

~Jeroen De Flander

PHINEHAS'S AXIOMS

- Nothing will happen to a dream you do nothing about.
- Greatness requires ongoing advancement from a life of mediocrity and obscurity to a life of significance.
- Your long-time accomplishments are a result of compounding short-term efforts.
- Your ability to move toward greatness and maximize your potential requires a developed ability to make great decisions.
- If you never attempt to make decisions for fear of making the wrong one, you cannot develop good decision-making skills.
- If you fail to put in the work of training yourself through the power of habit, you will fail to develop the capacity to emerge into greatness.
- Decision-making is not an easy straightforward process.
- Greatness is not birthed out of good intentions, but through consistent, positive habits.
- When people don't understand the level of your convictions, don't expect them to value your commitment to excellence.
- It's impossible to attain greatness without a commitment to excellence.
- Greatness is a process that demands patience and perseverance.
- Develop your mental and emotional fortitude to overcome the hardships that threaten your success, as you press on the path toward greatness.

- Your desire to manifest what you expect must be greater than the pain of the process, if you want to stay on the path to greatness.
- You must be totally dedicated to removing distractions and maintaining focus, if you desire to step into greatness.
- A distraction is not always a bad thing, but sometimes, it's a good thing at a wrong time.
- The key to advancement toward greatness is by rigorous execution of strategy through action.
- Greatness demands singleness of purpose and laser-like focus.
- I would rather have one dream that defines me, than many that are vague and unfulfilled.
- You cannot accomplish every good random idea and still be the greatest at one thing.
- Great people are remembered not because of the dreams they had, but for the ones they accomplished.

AFTERWORD

A great story is not just one linear story, but a sequence of events and plots, each scene building on the previous one and setting the stage for the next event. When woven together, the scenes form a fabric of the whole story in which we can make sense of the full plot. Your life's story is shaped by the layers of experiences, encounters, moments, information, insight, and motivation. It is these experiences that form the substratum of the chapters that later influence and define your life's story. No chapter in your life stands alone, for everything in your life is weaving a fabric that is telling your story.

Looking back over my life, I see different chapters that contribute to the telling of my story. This book is yet but another chapter of my life, an opportunity to continue to influence and empower people toward greatness. It could also be a turning point in your life, a resource that gives you keys to unlocking your greatness and writing the next chapter of your life.

I hope you have not only enjoyed this book, but also have been impacted by the tools and secrets I have shared. My desire is for you to grow and increase your capacity. To be more than you have ever been, to go further than you ever have, and to reach higher than you ever thought possible. These nine secrets I have offered you are not exhaustive of everything it takes to step into greatness, but they are extremely vital in initiating your journey on the path to greatness.

I believe that you chose this book, because you are eager to acquire the tools to make a difference and step into greatness. Whether or not you do anything today about this information that you have just acquired, the next five years will pass. Where will you be at the end of those five years? Will you have acted on what you learned? Or, will you still be where you are today? Is this book your opportunity to go for greatness? Or, will it sit collecting dust on your bookshelf?

Ask yourself:

- What is my responsibility with all this information I have acquired?
- Can I really do this? Am I ready to pay the price for greatness?
- Will I choose to act on and apply this information, so I can step into greatness, or is this just a lofty idea with no follow-through?
- Am I willing to start where I am today and engage these secrets daily to live intentionally, so I can move toward where I ought to be tomorrow?

Only you can decide if, when you come to your end of life, you will look back with regret, wishing and hoping you did something. Or, will you review your life with gratitude that you embraced this message and actualized your dreams? Stepping into greatness is not a destination, but a lifestyle.

From this moment on, choose to go about life armed with these secrets, determined that you will only have one aim—to bring significance and solutions to life, as you progressively step into greatness. Draw a line in the sand and say, "The buck stops with me, and my change starts right here and right now!"

This moment is reserved for those who will go beyond reading the book to applying the book and actualizing their dreams moving from dreaming to becoming. Begin living the chapters of this book and make this information count. I will see you at the TOP!

ABOUT THE AUTHOR

Phinehas Kinuthia is an international speaker, author, educator, life-coach, mentor, leader, and entrepreneur. His interest in pursuing new opportunities has led him through diverse careers, including real estate, insurance sales, small business, and entrepreneurship.

Phinehas's life is a compelling story that embodies his message that anyone can make their dreams a reality. Raised in poverty in Africa, he came to America with only $200 and a vision of unlimited possibility. He is an example that accomplishing dreams is possible. He is passionate about ordinary people discovering and living a life of purpose through accomplishing their dreams.

Phinehas is an expert on setting and achieving dreams. To the disenfranchised, Phinehas is a voice of hope and inspiration through speaking, books, coaching, and training. He conducts training workshops and offers programs to help people discover their purpose and teaches them how to pursue their dreams and live a full, passionate life of faith. He has taught people from different walks of life worldwide. His philosophy is that everyone possesses hidden treasure that is valuable only when it is discovered. He believes that you can be more than you are, go farther than you ever have, and reach higher than you ever thought possible.

Phinehas is also the Executive Global Liaison for ICN Human Rights Global Congress and a Golden Rule Goodwill Ambassador. He is a recipient of multiple awards, including President Girma Wolde-Giogis of Ethiopia Award as a Human Conservation Solutionist, The ICN Global Leadership Award, and ICN Life of Honor Award.

Phinehas is available for media appearances and speaking engagements. Learn more about his story and his programs. Be inspired to reach your dreams without limitation.

NOTES

CHAPTER 1

1. Phillip C. McGraw, PhD, *Self-Matters: Creating Your Life from the Inside Out* (Free Press, 2001).
2. "The Kalam Cosmological Argument," Philosophy of Religion, http://www.philosophyofreligion.info/theistic-proofs/the-cosmological-argument/the-kalam-cosmological-argument/.
3. Gene Veith, "Do you believe in Mother?" Patheos, February 9, 2015, http://www.patheos.com/blogs/geneveith/2015/02/do-you-believe-in-mother/.
4. Colossians 1:16, *The Message*.
5. Viktor E. Frankl, *Man's Search for Meaning* (New York, NY: Washington Square Press/Pocket Books, 1985).
6. Rick Warren, *The Purpose Driven Life: What on Earth Am I Here For?* (Grand Rapids, MI: Zondervan, 2012).

CHAPTER 2

1. Kendra Cherry, "Attitudes and Behavior in Psychology," Very Well Mind, October 31, 2017, http://psychology.about.com/od/socialpsychology/a/attitudes.htm.
2. John C. Maxwell, *Attitude 101: What Every Leader Needs to Know* (Nashville: Thomas Nelson, 2003).

3. Jeff Keller, *Attitude Is Everything: Change Your Attitude . . . Change Your Life!* (East Norwich, NY: Attitude Is Everything, 2012).

4. Philippians 4:11, *NKJV*.

CHAPTER 3

1. David Goldsmith and Lorrie Goldsmith, *Paid to Think: A Leader's Toolkit for Redefining Your Future* (Dallas, TX: BenBella Books, 2012).

2. Phinehas Kinuthia, *From Dreaming to Becoming* (Xulon Press, 2013).

3. James Allen, *As a Man Thinketh* (Trebecca Books).

4. John C. Maxwell, *Thinking for a Change: 11 Ways Highly Successful People Approach Life and Work* (New York: Center Street, 2005).

5. Gregory Berns, *Iconoclast: A Neuroscientist Reveals How to Think Differently* (Boston, MA: Harvard Business Press, 2010).

6. Carol S. Dweck, *Mindset: The New Psychology of Success* (New York: Ballantine Books, 2008).

7. Maxwell, *Thinking for a Change.*

8. Proverbs 13:20, *GNT*.

9. Philippians 4:8, *NKJV*.

10. Steve Jobs, Goodreads,
https://www.goodreads.com/quotes/653020-when-you-grow-up-you-tend-to-get-told-that.

11. Daniel H. Pink, *A Whole New Mind: Why Right-Brainers Will Rule the Future* (New York: Riverhead, 2006).

12. Blake Woolsey, "8 Characteristics of a Strategic Thinker," Mitchel, July 12, 2012,
http://blog.mitchcommgroup.com/blake/8-characteristics-of-a-strategic-thinker.

13. Maxwell, *Thinking for a Change*.

14. Donna Markova, PhD, and Angie McArthur, *Collaborative Intelligence: Thinking with People Who Think Differently* (New York: Spiegel & Grau, 2015).
15. Ibid.

CHAPTER 4

1. Proverbs 6:8, *NLT*.

2. Salim, Ismail, Michael S. Malone, and Yuri van Geest, *Exponential Organizations: Why New Organizations Are Ten Times Better, Faster, and Cheaper Than Yours (and What to Do about It)* (NY: Diversion Books, 2014), 29.

3. Rahul Gupta, "Nokia CEO ended his speech saying this 'we didn't do anything wrong, but somehow, we lost,'" LinkedIn, May 8, 2016,
https://www.linkedin.com/pulse/nokia-ceo-ended-his-speech-saying-we-didnt-do-anything-rahul-gupta/.

4. James M. Kouzes and Barry Z. Posner, *The Leadership Challenge: How to Make Extraordinary Things Happen in Organizations*, 5th ed. (Jossey Bass Inc., 2012).

5. Ismail, *Exponential Organizations*, 31.

6. General Stanley A. McChrystal, Tatum Collins, David Silverman, and Chris Fussell, *Team of Teams: New Rules of Engagement for a Complex World* (New York: Penguin Publishing Group, 2015), 20.

7. Greg Satell, "A Look Back at Why Blockbuster Really Failed and Why It Didn't Have To," *Forbes*, September 5, 2014, http://www.forbes.com/sites/gregsatell/2014/09/05/a-look-back-at-why-blockbuster-really-failed-and-why-it-didnt-have-to/#34947961261a.

8. Ibid.

9. Kinuthia, *From Dreaming to Becoming*.

10. McChrystal, *Team of Teams*.

11. Coach John Wooden, and Steve Jamison, *Wooden* (New York: Contemporary Books, 1997).

CHAPTER 5

1. Proverbs 22:15, *NKJV*.
2. Luke 6:31, *NIV*.
3. Proverbs 15:33b, *NKJV*.

CHAPTER 6

1. Kinuthia, *From Dreaming to Becoming*.

2. John C. Maxwell, *Everyone Communicates, Few Connect: What the Most Effective People Do Differently* (Nashville, TN: Thomas Nelson, 2010).

3. Paul W. Swets, *The Art of Talking So That People Will Listen: Getting Through to Family, Friends, and Business Associates* (New York: Simon & Schuster, 1992).
4. Stephen R. Covey, *The 7 Habits of Highly Effective People: Powerful Lessons in Personal Change* (New York: Simon & Schuster, 1989).
5. Peggy Noonan, *On Speaking Well: How to Give a Speech with Style, Substance and Clarity* (New York, Harper Collins, 1998).
6. Orrin Woodard, *Mentoring Matters: Targets, Techniques, and Tools for Becoming a Great Mentor* (Flint, MI: Obstacle Press, 2013).
7. Chris Brady, *Splash: A Leader's Guide to Effective Public Speaking* (Flint, MI: Obstacles Press, 2014).
8. Roger Fisher and William Ury, *Getting to Yes: Negotiating Agreement Without Giving In* (New York: Penguin Books, 2011).
9. Maxwell, *Everyone Communicates, Few Connect*.

10. Woodard, *Mentoring Matters*.
11. Oscar Amisi, *Generation Y: Engaging and Impacting This Generation* (Amisi, 2015).
12. James C. Humes, *The Sir Winston Method: The Five Secrets of Speaking the Language of Leadership* (New York: William Morrow & Company Inc, 1991).
13. Maxwell, *Everyone Communicates, Few Connect*.

14. Noonan, *On Speaking Well*.
15. Dale Carnegie, *The Quick and Easy Way to Effective Speaking: Modern Techniques for Dynamic Communication* (New York: Pocket Books, 1962).
16. Peter J. Daniels, *How to Have the Awesome Power of Public Speaking* (Australia: World Center of Entrepreneurial Studies Foundation, 1988).
17. Humes, *The Sir Winston Method*.
18. Jesse S. Nirenberg, PhD, *Getting Through to People* (Englewood Cliffs, N.J: Prentice-Hall, Inc., 1963).
19. Humes, *The Sir Winston Method*.
20. Noonan, *On Speaking Well*.
21. Dianna Boohner, *Creating Personal Presence: Look, Talk, Think, and Act Like a Leader* (San Francisco, CA: Berrett-Koehler Publishers, Inc., 2011).
22. Swets, *The Art of Talking*.
23. Carnegie, *The Quick and Easy Way to Effective Speaking*.

CHAPTER 7

1. Quoted in Dan Colman, "All You Need is Love: The Keys to Happiness Revealed by a 75-Year Harvard Study," February 9, 2015, http://www.openculture.com/2015/02/the-keys-to-happiness-revealed-by-a-75-year-long-harvard-study.html.

2. Proverbs 13:20, *NLT*.

3. Proverbs 27:17, *AMP*.

4. Van Moody, *The People Factor: How Building Great Relationships and Ending Bad Ones Unlocks Your God-Given Purpose* (Nashville, TN: Thomas Nelson, 2014).

5. George E. Vaillant, *Triumphs of Experience: The Men of the Harvard Grant Study* (Cambridge, MA: Belknap Press, 2012), quoted from "Grant Study," *Wikipedia*, https://en.wikipedia.org/wiki/Grant_Study#cite_note-7.

CHAPTER 8

1. Jimmy L. Collins, *Creative Followership: In the Shadow of Greatness* (Decatur, GA: Looking Glass Books, Inc., 2013).
2. Barbara Kellerman, *Followership: How Followers Are Creating Change and Changing Leaders* (Boston, MA: Harvard Business School Press, 2008).
3. Pat Mesiti, *Attitudes and Altitudes: The Dynamics of 21st Century Leadership* (Thornleigh, NSW: Pat Mesiti Ministries, 1997).
4. Collins, *Creative Followership*.
5. Seth Godin, *Tribes: We Need You to Lead Us* (New York: Portfolio, 2008).
6. https://www.goodreads.com/author/quotes/62012.Sheri_Dew.
7. Warren Bennis, *On Becoming a Leader* (New York: Basic Books, 2009).
8. Thomas J. Watson quoted in John Maxwell, *The Leadership Handbook: 26 Critical Lessons Every Leader Needs* (Nashville, TN: Thomas Nelson, 2015).
9. Carmine Gallo, "How Starbucks CEO Howard Schultz Inspired Us to Dream Bigger," *Forbes*, December 2, 2016, https://www.forbes.com/sites/carminegallo/2016/12/02/how-starbucks-ceo-howard-schultz-inspired-us-to-dream-bigger/#75d2bf41e858.
10. James M. Kouzes and Barry Z. Posner, *The Leadership Challenge: How to Make Extraordinary Things Happen in Organizations*, 5th ed. (Jossey Bass Inc., 2012).
11. Luke 9:61–62, *NLT*.

12. Jack Canfield, Mark Victor Hanson, and Anna Unkovich, *Chicken Soup for The Soul: In the Classroom* (Deerfield Park, FL: Health Communications, Inc., 2007).

13. John Maxwell, *Leadership Gold: Lessons Learned from a Lifetime of Leading* (Nashville, TN: Thomas Nelson, 2008).

14. Andy Stanley, *The Next Generation Leader: Five Essentials for Those Who Will Shape the Future* (Oregon: Multnomah Publishers, Inc., 2003).

15. Collins, *Creative Followership*.

16. Ibid.

17. Warren, *Purpose Driven Life*.

18. Stephen Covey, *The 7 Habits of Highly Effective People: Powerful Lessons in Life Change* (New York: Simon & Schuster, 1989).

CHAPTER 9

1. Jim Collins, *Good to Great* (New York, NY: Harper Business, 2001).

2. Bob Proctor, *The Art of Living* (New York, NY: Tarcher, 2016).

3. Zig Ziglar, "Priming the Pump," Leader Network.org, n.d., http://www.leadernetwork.org/Zig_Ziglar_Priming_the_Pump.htm.

4. Jeff Olson, *The Slight Edge: Turning Simple Disciplines into Massive Success* (Lake Dallas, TX: Success Books, 2013).

5. William Clement Stone, *The Success System That Never Fails* (Blacksburg, VA: Wilder Pub., 2010).

6. Pat Mesiti, *Attitudes and Altitudes: The Dynamics of 21st Century Leadership* (Thornleigh, NSW: Pat Mesiti Ministries, 1997).

7. Lewis Howes, *The School of Greatness: A Real-World Guide to Living Bigger, Loving Deeper, and Leaving a Legacy* (New York, NY: Rodale, 2015).

8. Zig Ziglar, *Better Than Good* (Brentwood, TN: Integrity, 2006).

9. Pat Riley, *The Winner Within: A Life Plan for Team Players* (New York, NY: Berkley Books, 1994).

10. Denis Waitley, "Autograph Your Career and Your Life with Excellence," Nightingale Conant, n.d., http://www.nightingale.com/articles/autograph-your-career-and-your-life-with-excellence/.

11. Samuel Chand, *Leadership Pain: The Classroom for Growth* (Nashville, TN: Thomas Nelson, 2015).

12. Angela Duckworth, *Grit: The Power of Passion and Perseverance* (New York, NY: Simon & Schuster, 2016).

13. Isaiah Berlin, "The Hedgehog and the Fox" quoted in Jim Collins, *Good to Great* (New York, NY: Harper Business, 2001).

14. Ibid.

15. Brian Dodd, *10 Indispensable Practices of the 2-Minute Leader* (Camarillo, CA, Spire Resources, 2013).

16. Chris McChesney, Sean Covey, and Jim Huling, *The 4 Disciplines of Execution: Achieving Your Wildly Important Goals* (New York, NY: Free Press, 2016).
Ibid.